LANGUAGE AND LITERACY SERIES

Dorothy S. Strickland, FOUNDING EDITOR
Celia Genishi and Donna E. Alvermann, SERIES EDITORS
ADVISORY BOARD: *Richard Allington, Kathryn Au, Bernice Cullinan, Colette Daiute,
Anne Haas Dyson, Carole Edelsky, Mary Juzwik, Susan Lytle, Django Paris, Timothy Shanahan*

continued

Language and Literacy Series, *continued*

Inspiring Dialogue
MARY M. JUZWIK ET AL.

Reading the Visual
FRANK SERAFINI

Race, Community, and Urban Schools
STUART GREENE

ReWRITING the Basics
ANNE HAAS DYSON

Writing Instruction That Works
ARTHUR N. APPLEBEE ET AL.

Literacy Playshop
KAREN E. WOHLWEND

Critical Media Pedagogy
ERNEST MORRELL ET AL.

A Search Past Silence
DAVID E. KIRKLAND

The ELL Writer
CHRISTINA ORTMEIER-HOOPER

Reading in a Participatory Culture
HENRY JENKINS ET AL., EDS.

Summer Reading
RICHARD L. ALLINGTON & ANNE MCGILL-FRANZEN, EDS.

Real World Writing for Secondary Students
JESSICA SINGER EARLY & MEREDITH DECOSTA

Teaching Vocabulary to English Language Learners
MICHAEL F. GRAVES ET AL.

Literacy for a Better World
LAURA SCHNEIDER VANDERPLOEG

Socially Responsible Literacy
PAULA M. SELVESTER & DEBORAH G. SUMMERS

Learning from Culturally and Linguistically Diverse Classrooms
JOAN C. FINGON & SHARON H. ULANOFF, EDS.

Bridging Literacy and Equity
ALTHIER M. LAZAR ET AL.

"Trust Me! I Can Read"
SALLY LAMPING & DEAN WOODRING BLASE

Reading Girls
HADAR DUBROWSKY MA'AYAN

Reading Time
CATHERINE COMPTON-LILLY

A Call to Creativity
LUKE REYNOLDS

Literacy and Justice Through Photography
WENDY EWALD ET AL.

The Successful High School Writing Center
DAWN FELS & JENNIFER WELLS, EDS.

Interrupting Hate
MOLLIE V. BLACKBURN

Playing Their Way into Literacies
KAREN E. WOHLWEND

Teaching Literacy for Love and Wisdom
JEFFREY D. WILHELM & BRUCE NOVAK

Overtested
JESSICA ZACHER PANDYA

Restructuring Schools for Linguistic Diversity, 2nd Ed.
OFELIA B. MIRAMONTES ET AL.

Words Were All We Had
MARÍA DE LA LUZ REYES, ED.

Urban Literacies
VALERIE KINLOCH, ED.

Bedtime Stories and Book Reports
CATHERINE COMPTON-LILLY & STUART GREENE, EDS.

Envisioning Knowledge
JUDITH A. LANGER

Envisioning Literature, 2nd Ed.
JUDITH A. LANGER

Writing Assessment and the Revolution in Digital Texts and Technologies
MICHAEL R. NEAL

Artifactual Literacies
KATE PAHL & JENNIFER ROWSELL

(Re)Imagining Content-Area Literacy Instruction
RONI JO DRAPER, ED.

Change Is Gonna Come
PATRICIA A. EDWARDS ET AL.

When Commas Meet Kryptonite
MICHAEL BITZ

Literacy Tools in the Classroom
RICHARD BEACH ET AL.

Harlem on Our Minds
VALERIE KINLOCH

Teaching the New Writing
ANNE HERRINGTON ET AL., EDS.

Children, Language, and Literacy
CELIA GENISHI & ANNE HAAS DYSON

Children's Language
JUDITH WELLS LINDFORS

Children's Literature and Learning
BARBARA A. LEHMAN

Storytime
LAWRENCE R. SIPE

Effective Instruction for Struggling Readers, K–6
BARBARA M. TAYLOR & JAMES E. YSSELDYKE, EDS.

The Effective Literacy Coach
ADRIAN RODGERS & EMILY M. RODGERS

Writing in Rhythm
MAISHA T. FISHER

Reading the Media
RENEE HOBBS

teaching**media***literacy*.com
RICHARD BEACH

What Was It Like?
LINDA J. RICE

Research on Composition
PETER SMAGORINSKY, ED.

New Literacies in Action
WILLIAM KIST

READING
THE
RAINBOW

LGBTQ-Inclusive Literacy Instruction in the Elementary Classroom

Caitlin L. Ryan
Jill M. Hermann-Wilmarth

Foreword by Mariana Souto-Manning

TEACHERS COLLEGE PRESS

TEACHERS COLLEGE | COLUMBIA UNIVERSITY

NEW YORK AND LONDON

GLSEN®

Published simultaneously by Teachers College Press, 1234 Amsterdam Avenue, New York, NY 10027, and GLSEN, 110 William Street, 30th Floor, New York, NY 10038.

GLSEN creates safe and inclusive schools for all. We envision a world in which every child learns to respect and accept all people, regardless of sexual orientation, gender identity, and/or expression. Each year, GLSEN programs and resources reach millions of students and educators in K-12 schools across the United States, and our network of 39 community-led chapters in 26 states brings GLSEN's expertise to local communities. GLSEN's progress and impact have won support for inclusive schools at all levels of education in the United States and sparked an international movement to ensure equality for LGBTQ students and respect for all in schools. For more information on GLSEN's policy advocacy, student leadership initiatives, public education, research, and educator training programs, please visit www.glsen.org.

Library of Congress Cataloging-in-Publication Data is available at loc.gov

ISBN 978-0-8077-5933-2 (paper)
ISBN 978-0-8077-7711-4 (ebook)

Printed on acid-free paper
Manufactured in the United States of America

25 24 23 22 21 20 19 18   8 7 6 5 4 3 2 1

This book is dedicated to Maree, Rose, and Barbara for welcoming us into their teaching and to queer people of all ages, who deserved and deserve more inclusive and equitable classrooms.

Contents

Foreword *Mariana Souto-Manning*   ix

Acknowledgments   xiii

1. **A Rationale for Teaching LGBTQ Topics
   in Elementary English Language Arts**   1

   LGBTQ Topics Matter to Elementary School Students
      and Their Families   4

   LGBTQ-Inclusion and English Language Arts Curricula
      Go Hand in Hand   8

   What You Will Find In This Book   11

**PART I: EXPANDING REPRESENTATIONS OF LGBTQ
   PEOPLE IN ELEMENTARY ENGLISH LANGUAGE ARTS**   17

2. **Introducing LGBTQ People Into Your Teaching**   19

   Why Representations Matter for Kids   20

   Doing the Work of Expanding Representations   22

   Considerations and Challenges in Your Context   34

3. **Expanding LGBTQ Representations Through
   Novel Studies**   37

   Teaching a Novel with a Gay Protagonist   39

   Teaching a Novel with a Transgender Protagonist   47

**PART II: QUESTIONING CATEGORIES BY READING
   STRAIGHT BOOKS THROUGH A QUEER LENS**   55

4. **Discussing Queer Moments in Straight Books**   57

   The Importance of Categories   58

   Doing the Work of Questioning Categories   61

   Considerations and Challenges in Your Context   71

5. **Building Students' Queer Lenses Through
    Anchor Lessons**   73

    Beginning Discussions of Unwritten Gender Rules   74

    Anchor Lessons as Touchstones for Continued Learning   77

    Using This Method With Another Anchor Text   81

**PART III: QUESTIONING SILENCES IN EXPANDED
REPRESENTATIONS**   83

6. **Acknowledging Silences in LGBTQ Inclusion**   85

    The Importance of Complicating "Single Story"
        Representations   86

    Doing the Work of Questioning Representations   88

    Considerations and Challenges in Your Context   96

7. **Connecting LGBTQ Characters and the Larger World**   98

    Teaching *After Tupac and D Foster*   99

    Specific and Intentional English Language Arts Teaching   103

**Conclusion: Mapping Out Your Journey—
Making a Plan and Finding Your Resources**   107

    Know Your Sources of Support   108

    Know Your Laws and Policies   109

    Making and Supporting Your Decisions   111

    Closing Thoughts   114

Appendix   117

    Classroom Materials   117

    Lesson Planning Materials   119

    Links to LGBTQ Glossaries   120

Children's Literature Cited   121

References   123

Index   131

About the Authors   139

Committing to Justice
Reading the Rainbow as a Right and Responsibility

Will you commit to justice in and through your teaching? This is the question at the heart of Caitlin Ryan's and Jill Hermann-Wilmarth's book, *Reading the Rainbow: LGBTQ-Inclusive Literacy Instruction in the Elementary Classroom*. In this book filled with powerful invitations and resources, Ryan and Hermann-Wilmarth, who were elementary school teachers before becoming teacher educators, invite us to enact justice in our classrooms as we honor our students' rights and work to foster equity. They offer a compelling rationale for LGBTQ inclusion in the elementary grades as a matter of justice.

Having engaged in LGBTQ-inclusive teaching in the primary grades in a public school in the South (Souto-Manning & Hermann-Wilmarth, 2008) and collaborated with teachers such as Dana Frantz Bentley (Bentley & Souto-Manning, 2016, 2018; Souto-Manning, 2013), who teaches pre-K in the Northeast, I know all too well that there are fears fueled by myths and misconceptions that often prevent teachers from discussing LGBTQ topics with young children. Although we educators tend to focus on whether children are ready, the real obstacle often preventing some of us from engaging in this work can be represented by the following question: Am *I* ready? I can't possibly talk about *sex* in the elementary school classroom. Rest assured that this book is not about sex education in the elementary classroom. Yet, if questions and concerns such as these have ever crossed your mind and prevented you from engaging in LGBTQ-inclusive teaching, you are in for a treat, as this book takes such issues and questions head on.

In this engaging and powerful book, Ryan and Hermann-Wilmarth explain that LGBTQ-inclusive teaching means acknowledging the humanity of LGBTQ individuals and communities. Through a number of rich and diverse examples from elementary classrooms, they make visible how elementary teachers have negotiated LGBTQ-inclusive teaching, shedding light onto possibilities for us to engage in LGBTQ-inclusive teaching and learning in our own classrooms. They make visible how LGBTQ-inclusive curriculum and teaching are not "add-ons" or "extras;" they are instead invitations to re-envision well-known curricular structures such as read-alouds, book discussions, and writing workshops.

In addition to identifying a number of wonderful resources (throughout the book and in the Appendix), Ryan and Hermann-Wilmarth also offer new ways of engaging with existing resources as a pathway for LGBTQ-inclusive teaching. They show, for example, how books in the Harry Potter series can be repositioned to foster LGBTQ-inclusive literacy teaching and learning. This is not to say that there are no obstacles to doing LGBTQ-inclusive teaching; there are. And Ryan and Hermann-Wilmarth address these throughout this book, in sections aptly entitled "Considerations and Challenges in Your Context." After reading this book, I am convinced that you will not be able to find an excuse to sanction the exclusion and invisibilization of LGBTQ individuals, communities, histories, and issues from the elementary classroom.

But since you haven't yet started reading the powerful book ahead of you, you may still be questioning why you should dedicate the time and effort to engage in reading this book and then in "reading the rainbow" in your own classroom. I propose that "reading the rainbow," or LGBTQ inclusion in the elementary classroom, is not a privilege or an option; it is a right and a responsibility. Let me explain. A right is defined as "being in accordance to what is just;" as such, it rests on equity. It is the right of our students to see themselves, their families, and their communities represented and included. It is also the right of students who do not belong to LGBTQ families and communities to learn about diversities within the world in which they live in ways that don't deny anyone's humanity and that don't foster stereotypes. The denial of such a right is inequitable, unethical, and harmful (causing possible emotional and psychological harm; see NAEYC, 2011). Quite simply, it fosters injustice in and through teaching.

It is our responsibility as teachers to commit to LGBTQ-inclusive teaching and to foster equitable classrooms. After all, as Ryan and Hermann-Wilmarth propose, in equitable classrooms, "all students are encouraged to learn about the diverse world around them in more nuanced and expansive ways" (p. 1). Ryan and Hermann-Wilmarth urge us to embrace our responsibility as educators to question the silences in our classrooms, in the materials we use, and even in the expanded representations we bring to the classroom.

As you engage in this soon-to-begin wondrous learning journey, I hope you will fully engage and take Ryan's and Hermann-Wilmarth's invitations to stop and think about what each chapter means to you by considering the "Stop and Think" questions they offer throughout the book. They will help you envision ways of getting started or to expand your current approach to LGBTQ-inclusive teaching. They are rooted in the belief that "everyone can do *something* to make their classrooms more inclusive" (p. 12). But most of all, I sincerely hope that you will commit to fostering justice in and through your teaching. Why? In the words of a then 4-year-old preschooler, who is now an elementary school student: "That's fair and that's how it works" (Bentley & Souto-Manning, 2016, p. 195).

—Mariana Souto-Manning
Teachers College, Columbia University

REFERENCES

Bentley, D. F., & Souto-Manning, M. (2016). Toward inclusive understandings of marriage in an early childhood classroom: Negotiating (un)readiness, community, and vulnerability through a critical reading of "King and King." *Early Years: An International Journal of Research and Development, 36*(2), 195–206.

Bentley, D. F., & Souto-Manning, M. (2018). "We were marching for our equal rights": Political literacies in the early childhood classroom. In N. Yelland & D. F. Bentley (Eds.), *Found in translation: Connecting reconceptualist thinking with early childhood education practices* (pp. 91–110). New York, NY: Routledge.

National Association for the Education of Young Children (NAEYC). (2011). *NAEYC code of ethical conduct and statement of commitment.* Retrieved from www.naeyc.org/files/naeyc/image/public_policy/Ethics%20Position%20Statement2011_09202013update.pdf

Souto-Manning, M. (2013). *Multicultural teaching in the early childhood classroom: Strategies, tools, and approaches, Preschool–2nd grade.* Washington, DC: Association for Childhood Education International and New York, NY: Teachers College Press.

Souto-Manning, M., & Hermann-Wilmarth, J. M. (2008). Teacher inquiries into gay and lesbian families in early childhood classrooms. *Journal of Early Childhood Research, 6*(3), 263–280.

Acknowledgments

Writing a book in a collaborative team, across states, requires much coordination and support. We are incredibly grateful for the multiple communities who have advocated for the teaching, research, and writing that have culminated in this book.

Maree, Rose, and Barbara not only opened their classroom doors, but shared their planning time, commiserated at the end of challenging days, and celebrated with us as we watched kids build new understandings. Presenting with them and about their classrooms at conferences helped us refine ideas, revise lesson plans, and shape our writing. The teaching and learning they continue to do with their students gives us hope. This book would not exist if not for them.

This work was generously supported by the College of Education, the Graduate School, and the Department of Literacy Studies, English Education, and History Education at East Carolina University, as well as the College of Education and Human Development, the Department of Teaching, Learning, and Educational Studies, and the Tate Grant and Innovation Center at Western Michigan University.

We are grateful to Teachers College Press for giving this book a home, especially Acquisitions Editor Emily Spangler, and to GLSEN for their co-publishing support. Knowing this book would be a resource in GLSEN's workshops and trainings made our work better.

Many colleagues have supported our thinking around this project over the years. Mollie Blackburn is a friend and mentor who has generously encouraged our thinking and helped us navigate the challenge of writing our first book. Mariana Souto-Manning's teaching, scholarship, and advice have been important influences on us for years. We are grateful she could lend her voice to this book, both in the Foreword and through the glimpses we share of her 2nd-grade classroom in Chapter 2. We first read Janine Schall and Gloria Kauffmann's groundbreaking work when we were graduate students. It continues to make a difference in our thinking about what kind of LGBTQ-inclusive ELA teaching is possible in elementary classrooms.

Our lives are made better by the friends and family who inspire us, encourage us, and help us believe in this work on the days when it's hard.

Caitlin is especially grateful for her incredible networks of support that stretch across North Carolina, Ohio, and beyond. You know who you are. Your phone calls, voice mails, visits, and book clubs make life much more fun. She thanks her parents for their love and for living in a state between North Carolina and Michigan where she and Jill could meet up to write. And most of all, she thanks Allison for loving her, for laughing with her, and for always being by her side.

Jill has been inspired to find ways to create LGBTQ-inclusive ELA classrooms by her children since before they were born, and is grateful for their eye rolls and cheers all these years later. She especially thanks Jessica for all of it.

READING
THE
RAINBOW

CHAPTER 1

A Rationale for Teaching LGBTQ Topics in Elementary English Language Arts

After over a decade of teaching and research, we believe elementary school English language arts (ELA) curriculum can include lesbian, gay, bisexual, transgender, and queer (LGBTQ) topics. We're convinced that this kind of inclusive teaching can help create more equitable classrooms where LGBTQ students and their families are treated equally and all students are encouraged to learn about the diverse world around them in more nuanced and expansive ways. If you're like many of the hundreds of pre- and inservice teachers we've worked with over the last several years, hearing those statements might raise a number of questions in your mind: Can elementary-school-age students really talk about LGBTQ topics? What would that teaching actually look like? How would that work for me where I teach? Would I need permission from parents or administrators to do that kind of work? Aren't topics like LGBTQ rights and visibility better left to parents to clarify for their children? And, really, isn't talking about these topics in elementary school too early? Shouldn't those be topics middle or high school teachers address instead? What good will it do to bring such controversial topics into the classrooms of such young children? And even if I wanted to try LGBTQ-inclusive teaching, where would it fit in my already overscheduled teaching day?

These are the very real questions that this book will address. First, we will explain why the realities of diversity, both in our schools and in the larger world, make it important to talk about LGBTQ topics with young children, even for readers who still have some questions or concerns about doing that. Then, by looking at three different approaches to integrating LGBTQ topics and people into ELA curriculum, we will help readers identify different methods they can match to their comfort level and context. We use examples of LGBTQ-inclusive ELA teaching taken from a range of elementary school classroom settings to illustrate these approaches.

Questions and concerns about LGBTQ-inclusive teaching often stem from cultural myths and misconceptions about LGBTQ people, leading some to think it is never okay to discuss LGBTQ topics with children, particularly not in schools. Often, this concern rests on the fear that talking about LGBTQ topics means talking about sex, and that, understandably, makes teachers feel uncomfortable at best. When we consider talking to children about LGBTQ people, however, we mean something very different. If we shift our understanding of LGBTQ people away from sex and toward who people are, including how they live, whom they love, and with whom they build family and community, these discussions become a lot more relevant. Rather than thinking about "controversial issues," we are thinking about people in our students' lives, and maybe even our students themselves. We can also think about LGBTQ inclusion in terms of how we treat each other, how we live in a diverse community, and how we understand our common humanity, even across differences. With this shift in perspective around the reasons for discussing LGBTQ identities, we can start to see how these topics actually might have a place not just in schools generally but in elementary schools in particular.

We are aware that some people go so far as to deny the humanity of LGBTQ people and are therefore entirely unwilling to consider LGBTQ-inclusive education under any circumstance. However, we believe the number of teachers who think this way is actually quite small. We know many more teachers who have simply never thought about these questions before. Others have never considered an overlap between LGBTQ people and their mandated curricular content, so they don't see how addressing LGBTQ topics needs to go beyond just stopping homophobic bullying. We also know teachers who worry about saying the wrong thing, so they stay silent around LGBTQ topics to prevent making mistakes. Other teachers work in schools where the administrators or school district policies prevent them from feeling free to discuss LGBTQ topics and keep their jobs. This fear may be especially strong in times where the larger political context is less friendly to LGBTQ people. But we also have met teachers who want to teach in LGBTQ-inclusive ways, but have no idea how to get started since they haven't seen models of what this could look like in our current educational climate. And some of the readers of this text, like the teachers profiled in this book, may already include LGBTQ topics or books in their classrooms but are always looking for more ideas.

We want this book to provide teachers possessing a range of experiences and beliefs with tools for addressing LGBTQ topics in their ELA teaching because, after having spent time in schools as students, as teachers, and now as researchers, we know that LGBTQ topics are relevant to the lives of children and teachers in elementary schools and classrooms. Consider, for example, the following scenarios. Have you seen similar events or could you imagine yourself as the teacher when one of these occurs?

You're on lunch duty when you see a group of 3rd-grade boys carrying their trays pause near a 1st-grade boy who is sitting with several girls. They taunt him: "Sitting with the girls? Ew! What are you? Gay? I bet your favorite color is pink!" You send them off to their seats, but you wonder how to help the bullied student and the students doing the bullying. Maybe you wonder how you can help them understand how colors and friends don't determine if you're gay or whether you're a boy or a girl.

You're excited to find a book by award-winning author Patricia Polacco that you hadn't seen before. You see it's called *In Our Mothers' House* and has two women and several children on the front. You wonder if it's appropriate for kids or if you would even be allowed to read this book about lesbian moms in your 2nd-grade classroom. You wonder: What would my principal say? What would my students say? What would my students' parents say? Is it worth it when you could just find another book instead?

Your principal tells you that next week you'll have a new student in your kindergarten class. The student, she explains, will be listed on your roster as a girl named Janna, but that this child now identifies as a boy and is called John. You aren't sure how you will address this. You're particularly worried because you make a point to include your children's identities in the curriculum; how could you possibly find materials that would address John's experience? How will you answer the other children's questions?

The kids in your classroom are talking about the gay couple on the popular network sitcom *Modern Family*. They don't sound mean, but it's clear they find the idea of a male couple, especially a male couple with kids, to be unusual and somewhat uncomfortable. You know that there is a student in the other 5th-grade class with two dads, and you wonder how that student would feel if he heard your students' talk. You wonder if you should tell them to stop, ignore them, or if maybe you could build on your students' enjoyment of and knowledge of the show to help them explore the homophobic remarks you sometimes hear from them on the playground and in the more casual spaces of the classroom about LGBTQ people being different or strange.

From these scenarios, and many others that might now be in your mind, you can see that topics relating to gender and sexuality already show up in elementary school classrooms. In other words, this means that explicitly addressing LGBTQ topics does not "add" or "bring" sexuality into the curriculum. Rather, including LGBTQ topics in a systematic, teacher-led way just ensures that these categories are talked about more inclusively so that more people are represented.

After all, students learn about gender and sexuality from their teachers long before they take a formal sex education class. Messages about gender and sexuality, both implicit and explicit, are everywhere in elementary schools (Blaise, 2005; DePalma & Atkinson, 2009; Kehily, 2004; Renold, 2005; Robinson, 2005; Ryan, 2016; Wallace & VanEvery, 2000; Wohlwend, 2009). Sometimes these messages are conveyed through the words we use, like calling a teacher "Mrs." to show she's married or when a female teacher uses the term "my husband" in conversation. When teachers use a mock wedding scenario to teach children how Q and U always go together, they reference sexuality through the use of the adult (gendered and sexualized) activity of marriage. Sometimes gender and sexuality are highlighted when we say "boys and girls" or when we have children line up in girl- and boy-segregated lines. Many times sexuality shows up in the texts we read: multiple stories with a mom and a dad, where children are traditionally masculine boys and feminine girls, and fairy tales where princes always kiss princesses and live happily ever after. And sometimes it happens through the things children talk about: their gay uncle, their favorite lesbian character on a popular television show, or their disgust at a girl who wants to play with the boys on the playground.

Yet, even when teachers recognize these kinds of scenarios as communicating a particular view of gender and sexuality, they may not understand the power they have to step in and expand these perspectives to make room for more of their students, nor realize what kinds of teaching might be possible in response to such situations. They are afraid of violating policies, saying the "wrong" thing, not having the answers to questions, offending families with opposing beliefs, and, of course, getting fired. They wonder how principals, parents, and students might react, and when they could even find the time to do one more thing in an already-packed school year. They don't know if they can take time away from the curriculum that their students will be tested on to make topics of gender and sexuality a feature in their teaching, especially if they don't see how these topics are directly relevant to their classrooms. Given these realities, it is important for teachers to have a rationale for *why* an LGBTQ-inclusive curriculum is important for the students they serve. We invite you to enter this journey wherever you are, doing what you can to create LGBTQ-inclusive classrooms for the benefit of all your students.

LGBTQ TOPICS MATTER
TO ELEMENTARY SCHOOL STUDENTS AND THEIR FAMILIES

Including LGBTQ topics in elementary schools is about much more than a push for political correctness. Above all, doing so makes a positive difference in the learning environment of a wide variety of students. Including LGBTQ topics in elementary classrooms allows students to see a wider range of people as important enough to be included in the curriculum. Statistics from GLSEN, an education organization working to create safe and inclusive schools for LGBTQ youth, indicate that such adjustments to curriculum matter. For example, they found that "75.2% of LGBTQ students in schools with an inclusive curriculum said their peers were accepting of LGBTQ people, compared to 39.6% of those without an inclusive curriculum" (Kosciw, Greytak, Giga, Villenas, & Danischewski, 2016, p. 8). This suggests that student behavior toward LGBTQ people is more welcoming in the presence of more inclusive instruction. We want to help readers build a general recognition of how LGBTQ-inclusive teaching can have a broad, positive impact on many different students, as we outline below. We believe that wider understanding about the many benefits of LGBTQ-inclusive curriculum for students can provide the best defense against possible resistance.

Students with LGBTQ Families

First of all, including LGBTQ topics in elementary school classrooms is important to do for the many children with LGBTQ parents and family members. There are an estimated 6 million people with one or more LGBTQ parents (Gates, 2014); at least 300,000 of those children are currently of school age (Adams & Persinger, 2013). Children with LGBTQ parents live in nearly every county in every state. As of 2013, Mississippi was the state with the highest percentage of LGBTQ couples raising children, while metro areas with the highest percentage of LGBTQ couples raising children include unlikely places such as Grand Forks, ND; Hinesville, GA; and Laredo, TX. Among larger metro areas of over a million people, the list of those with the highest percentage of LGBTQ couples with children includes similarly unlikely places such as Salt Lake City, UT; Virginia Beach, VA; Memphis, TN; Detroit, MI; and San Antonio, TX (Gates, 2015). This means that classrooms all over the country need to be prepared to teach children with LGBTQ parents and family members.

Research from GLSEN shows that elementary schools are not serving these children well (GLSEN & Harris Interactive, 2012). While we know that the connection between a child's home and school is an important support for a child's learning (Souto-Manning, 2013; Vasquez, 2004), only half of elementary school teachers (49%) say an elementary school student with a lesbian, gay, or bisexual parent would feel comfortable at the school where they teach, and only 42% think that would be true for a student with a transgender parent (GLSEN & Harris Interactive, 2012). Even though most teachers address family diversity generally, only two in ten elementary school students (18%) actually learn about families with two moms or two dads (GLSEN & Harris Interactive, 2012). This silence sends a message to children with LGBTQ parents that their families are not "real" families and that, certainly, their families are not accepted in the school. Even children as young as 6 from LGBTQ-headed households sometimes change their artwork, stories, family trees, and other kinds of family-related assignments in schools to hide their family identity (Ryan, 2010a).

Think about it: Could you talk about your family, even for just 30 seconds, while not giving away any information about the people's genders? It's really challenging! This is the kind of work students with LGBTQ parents have to do when they don't know whether their families are welcome in their schools. Luckily, when teachers and other adults in schools take time to include and show their respect for LGBTQ families, it makes a difference for these children's comfort in their classrooms (Ryan, 2010a). They can stop censoring themselves and instead be honest about the people they live with and love, focusing on being kids and learning rather than on hiding or making other people feel comfortable with their families. When other students see that teachers value LGBTQ-headed families, they also have a model for respect and can follow their lead (Souto-Manning & Hermann-Wilmarth, 2008).

Students Who Identify as LGBTQ

Including LGBTQ topics in elementary school classrooms is important to do for children who are LGBTQ-identified themselves, whether they come out while they are young or, more commonly, later in life. After all, every LGBTQ adult—over 4.1% of the nation's total population according to Gallup surveys from 2016 (Gates, 2017)—was once a school-age child. Unfortunately, as GLSEN's studies show (GLSEN & Harris Interactive, 2012; Kosciw et al., 2016), many of those children often witnessed their teachers staying silent while other students used the term "gay" in hateful ways. Sometimes they even heard teachers say these things themselves, and they almost never saw LGBTQ people included in the curriculum. On the other hand, many LGBTQ adults still remember those teachers who were committed to addressing these topics. They noticed whether or not their teachers thought gay people were deserving of respect, and they remembered that as they came out. As queer people ourselves, the language around LGBTQ people that our teachers used is certainly a part of our school memories and is likely one reason we find this work so important. What teachers do and say about these topics can have implications for years to come.

Elementary schools, specifically, are also being affected by increased awareness about the lives and needs of transgender children. These children have been assigned one gender at birth but, sometimes as early as 3 years old (Brill & Pepper, 2008; Leibowitz & Spack, 2011), consistently and persistently insist they are actually a different gender (American Academy of

Pediatrics, 2015; Meier & Harris, n.d.). Pediatric and psychological recommendations suggest, and recent research findings confirm, that supporting the gender identity a child asserts is an important part of healthy development (American Academy of Pediatrics, 2015; Meier & Harris, n.d.; Olson, Durwood, DeMeules, & McLaughlin, 2016; Substance Abuse and Mental Health Services Administration, 2014). This means elementary schools should be ready to affirm transgender children and their families in order to support children's mental health and development.

Students Who Are Harassed for Being LGBTQ

Including LGBTQ topics in elementary school classrooms is important to do for children who are harassed for their gender or sexuality even when they *aren't* LGBTQ-identified. Because LGBTQ people have historically been feared, hated, marginalized, bullied, and discriminated against, words to describe those who are LGBTQ are used as a way to shame people of all identities. This is why a little boy who is sensitive or doesn't like sports might be called a *fag* or a *sissy* or *gay* and why a little girl who is assertive or doesn't like dolls might be called a *dyke* or a *lesbo*. These words, especially when used by children against children, aren't meant to name a boy who is in love with another boy or a girl who is in love with another girl. Instead, they are used as a way to name and condemn behaviors that fall outside of the norm. In these cases, the children being harassed may or may not end up identifying as LGBTQ, but they are still bullied by association. These children benefit from learning in classrooms where teachers expand ideas of what girls and boys can do, in part by addressing LGBTQ topics in respectful ways. Readers interested in addressing these issues around gender and gender boundaries can see how other teachers approach this in Part II.

And Everyone Else Too

Lastly, including LGBTQ topics in elementary school classrooms is important to do for all children because we all live in a world with LGBTQ people. Children—even if they have a mom and a dad, identify as straight, and fit gender norms—will encounter LGBTQ people in their families, schools, workplaces, and communities. When teachers implement a curriculum that ignores these realities, students are left on their own to process what they hear about LGBTQ people in popular culture and learn respectful language for talking about LGBTQ topics. Perhaps this is the reason why it is in schools and classrooms where the humanity of LGBTQ people is ignored through curricular silences that bullying around LGBTQ identities is most likely to occur (Kosciw et al., 2016). Just as White people must be invested in ending racism and men must stand up for women's rights, non-LGBTQ people have an important role to play in making the world safer for and more inclusive of LGBTQ folks. Schools teach children about the world and equip students to live in it; that world includes LGBTQ people, and therefore schools should include LGBTQ topics.

LGBTQ-INCLUSION AND ENGLISH LANGUAGE ARTS CURRICULA GO HAND IN HAND

If including LGBTQ topics is, as we have argued, a good idea for all our students, how does that happen? Certainly, schools could examine their policies and procedures to address ways in which LGBTQ people and families are currently being excluded or diminished. Administrators could include LGBTQ people in anti-bullying policies. Teachers could use more-inclusive language when talking about families, such as saying "parents" or "grown-ups" rather than defaulting to "mom and dad." GLSEN and Welcoming Schools both focus specifically on how schools can become more inclusive places for LGBTQ students and families, and have freely accessible resources (see www.GLSEN.org and www.welcomingschools.org). We discuss these and other resources in our Conclusion chapter. But everyday classroom teaching is also an important opportunity for this work, especially because attending a school with inclusive curriculum is related to fewer hostile school experiences and increased feelings of connectedness to the school community for LGBTQ students (Kosciw, Greytak, Bartkiewicz, Boesen, & Palmer, 2012; Kosciw et al., 2016). Rather than finding one-time additive ways or special days for LGBTQ inclusion, we believe that there is a natural fit for ongoing LGBTQ inclusion in the English language arts curriculum.

From our own time teaching in elementary schools and from the work we do with both pre- and inservice teachers, we know how much content (and pressure!) is already loaded into the language arts curriculum. Things like levels and test scores and benchmark assessment data continue to shape daily literacy instruction for teachers and students. The Common Core and other standards stretch the amount of information we teach and the depth with which we teach it. We know teachers are working to find ways to engage kids in reading so that they are fluent, can identify a main idea, and can write a topic sentence. This, no doubt, is hard work. How in the world can teachers fit *more* teaching into their limited time with students?

While the idea of infusing curriculum with LGBTQ topics might seem overwhelming, new, or like yet another addition to a job with constant demands to do more, we will show how the work that teachers are already doing in the English language arts (ELA) is ripe for this infusion. We will help teachers combine the teaching they already do with a broader sense of who is included in that pedagogy.

Picture a great ELA classroom in your mind. Maybe it's yours! Maybe it's what you hope yours might look like one day. What do you see? You might think of students being deeply engaged in reading a wide variety of texts with choices about what they read and how they respond to that reading. You might think of student responses to texts that involve critical thinking skills and the highest levels of Bloom's taxonomy. You might think of curricular themes or integrated units or multigenre text sets where students synthesize their knowledge across a wide range of sources and demonstrate that knowledge through a variety of assessments. You might think of teachers who know their students as individuals and actively coach them at their instructional level in their zone of proximal development in ways that respond to their diverse needs. You might think of engaged dialogue where students' discussions of informational texts help them understand the larger world around them and where students' inquiries about fictional characters help them connect to their own lives and deepen their understandings of themselves and the spaces they inhabit in and out of school.

Now imagine that classroom as inclusive of LGBTQ topics.

While it might feel like a drastic shift, we believe that the only difference is an expansion of a teacher's way of thinking that includes a more diverse range of texts and topics. Below, we offer a few ways to think about those connections and possibilities.

Reading Is About Identity

Effective ELA teachers know that reading is about much more than just sounding out words. When we read, we bring together what we know and what we believe with what is in the text. Reading, therefore, is a transaction (Rosenblatt, 1938, 1956) between a reader and a text in a particular context. Seeing reading in this way acknowledges that literacy is intimately tied to our complex and complicated identities (Dutro, Kazemi, & Balf, 2006; Gadsden, 1993; Jones, 2012; Moje, Luke, Davies, & Street, 2009); what and how we read is mediated by our experiences. Picture, for example, what you think of when you read the word "dog." What comes to mind? A slobbery-but-adorable bulldog? A gentle golden retriever? The mascot of your college? Clifford the Big Red Dog? Do you think of happy memories of walks with your favorite pet? Scary memories of getting bitten? Images of police dogs who were set upon protesters during the civil rights movement? Even if we all decode the word the same way, our experiences shape the layers we bring to the word's meaning. The word "family" works in similar ways. Children with LGBTQ parents picture particular ideas of family, children with straight married parents imagine other images, and children who live in any number of other family configurations, still others. Therefore, when we make our ELA classrooms

LGBTQ-inclusive, we are allowing students to draw on all of who they and their families are to build their comprehension in order to be successful ELA students.

Additionally, when readers read, they don't just "take" meaning from a text; they actively construct their understanding. They do this in part individually, but also in active ways with one another (Britton, 1970). If you're a teacher who does any kind of book clubs or literature circles in your classroom, you've probably seen this in action. These types of discussions entail synthesis and negotiation of multiple points of view, all of which require higher-level thinking skills (Daniels, 2002). It's through this talk that students process and share what they know, hear from others, and continue to deepen their understandings of texts, themselves, and the world around them. It's this kind of reading and literacy that we are thinking of in this book—literacy that is meaning-focused, meaningful, generative, and builds on the lives of students and teachers, including when those lives involve LGBTQ people. When considered this way, literacy instruction invites the inclusion of LGBTQ people and topics. This brings LGBTQ topics into the classroom through literacy learning.

The Power of Story

Anyone who has ever sat and read a beloved book with a child knows just how captivating stories can be. We use stories, both as children and adults, to sort through our experiences and bring meaning to our world (Dyson & Genishi, 1994). Stories help us think about the actions and emotions of ourselves and others. They help us understand the things we deal with in our everyday lives and help us imagine worlds that are far away or entirely imaginary. They help us imagine a wide variety of possibilities for ourselves through their casts of characters and fanciful settings.

As people, we need to see ourselves in stories. We like that feeling of saying, "Look, there I am!" On the other hand, if we saw only ourselves all the time, our worlds would be limited to what we already know. We could get more than a bit narcissistic seeing only ourselves day after day. If, conversely, we are always learning about the worlds of others, we can feel lonely. We might understand that our view of the world is not the only one, but if we don't feel that there's a place in that world for us, then we can easily feel strange, isolated, and vulnerable. Just as readings of diverse books are important for students of various racial, ethnic, religious, socioeconomic, and ability groups (Dutro, 2001, 2009; Emdin, 2016; Enciso, 2004; Harris, 1992; Jones, 2006; Ladson-Billings, 1995; Morrell, 2007; Souto-Manning, 2013; Tyson, 1999), they are also important when it comes to LGBTQ people and topics.

Building Tools for Communicating and Creating Change

ELA teaching equips students with skills for communicating about a variety of topics in various genres for different audiences. This means the methods you use every day in your ELA classroom to help students become literate are the same tools that you would use as an LGBTQ-inclusive ELA teacher. The teaching of these ideas could be done as you teach students about the skills, strategies, and practices of reading and writing, speaking and listening, and viewing and visually representing. Students can, for example, compare and contrast characters from LGBTQ-inclusive books. Teachers can talk with guided reading groups about text-to-world connections and multiple meanings of Tier 2 words in a discussion of a newspaper article about local LGBTQ community events or anti-discrimination ordinances. Teachers can teach the distinctions between active and passive voice during writing workshop where students are writing about their diverse families or the diverse families in their school. Because ELA is the place where students learn these skills, they can be applied and further developed in a context of LGBTQ-inclusivity.

We help students develop literacy skills so they can engage with and act on the world around them. Because reading, writing, and oral language matter outside of the classroom, these skills are important to teach inside the classroom. This can mean involving students in using their literacy to question the way things are or the way things "have always been" to build a deeper understanding of people, power, cultural norms, and social inequalities (Cowhey, 2006; Dozier, Johnston, & Rogers, 2006; Freire, 1970/1994; Gatto, 2013; Janks, 2000; Lewison, Flint, & Van Sluys, 2002). When teachers help students look for and critique literature in which some fictional characters are more vulnerable than others and why that might be, they prepare students to apply those lessons to their own world. When students learn to recognize these patterns of inclusion and exclusion, they can also speak back to them, using their language and literacy skills to share their views, notice injustices, and create change. When applied to topics related to gender and sexuality, students' literacy has the potential to create spaces that are more welcoming and open to LGBTQ people.

WHAT YOU WILL FIND IN THIS BOOK

In this book we, as authors, are building on your ELA expertise. We know that you learned about reading comprehension, vocabulary, writing strategies, and many other methods in the teacher preparation program that you are currently in, that you recently graduated from, or that is a long way in your rearview mirror. Some of you have more daily practice under your belt than others. But you are all teachers who understand the importance of good ELA teaching, and have some ideas about what that looks like. We want to revisit those approaches with a new lens in mind that could help you include people that have often been silenced in elementary curriculum.

We know that teachers are different and enact their ELA curriculum differently, depending on a complicated mix of their own identities and the expectations of the school, district, and state in which they teach. This book acknowledges the intersections of those factors by offering multiple ways to bring LGBTQ ideas and concepts into ELA teaching. Because we also believe that no matter the restrictions, everyone can do *something* to make their classrooms more inclusive, we will explain different strategies to try. In this way, we hope to shift the conversation away from what you *can't* do to what you *could* do. Instead of considering *if* you can include particular lessons or particular texts in your instruction, we want to help you discover *how* you might find multiple, creative ways to address systems that exclude LGBTQ people. We will share portraits of teachers in multiple contexts using different approaches to LGBTQ inclusion so you can see how it *really* looks in a classroom and, therefore, how it might look in yours. We hope you will find different combinations of methods, tools, and theories that fit with who you are and the context in which you teach.

The Voices and Teachers in This Book

The people you'll hear from in this book, including both of the authors, are all current or former elementary school teachers. The real-life examples of teaching across a range of contexts are drawn primarily from three classrooms where LGBTQ-inclusive teaching was integrated into ELA curriculum. In addition to these focal teachers, we also venture into other classrooms whose teachers have shared their LGBTQ-inclusive elementary ELA work over the past decade in academic publications. These additional classrooms help us see how this teaching plays out in other regions of the country and in other grade levels.

Throughout our thinking, planning, and writing, the work we do is nested with and built upon other LGBTQ-inclusive classroom work in multiple contexts, across multiple grades, over a wide span of years, and using a variety of approaches (Athanases, 1996; Blackburn, 2002, 2003, 2005; Blackburn & Buckley, 2005; Blackburn, Clark, Kenney, & Smith, 2010; Blaise, 2005; Casper & Schultz, 1999; Clark & Blackburn, 2009; DePalma & Atkinson 2006, 2009; Epstein, 2000; Letts & Sears, 1999; Meyer, Tilland-Stafford, & Airton, 2016; Payne & Smith, 2012; Pinar, 1998; Quinlivan & Town, 1999; Robinson, 2005; Schall & Kauffmann, 2003; Sumara & Davis, 1998). These studies, and likely many others, have informed the field of LGBTQ-inclusive teaching and helped build a foundation for our contribution to it.

The Authors. We, Caitlin and Jill, each taught elementary school in grades ranging from K through 5, in a variety of contexts before becoming teacher educators. In our current roles as university professors, we teach teachers about literacy, language arts, children's literature, diversity, and social justice. We also conduct research, which for us means collaborating with practicing teachers to see how the ideas that we teach about at the university level work with real kids in real classrooms. Our focus over the last several years has been planning and documenting LGBTQ-inclusive ELA teaching in elementary school classrooms. This research has helped us think about the theories behind these ideas (Hermann-Wilmarth & Ryan, 2015a, 2016; Hermann-Wilmarth & Souto-Manning, 2007; Ryan & Hermann-Wilmarth, 2013), what makes some texts better to use than others in certain kinds of lessons (Hermann-Wilmarth, 2007; Hermann-Wilmarth & Ryan, 2015a, 2015b, 2016), how this teaching makes a difference for students with LGBTQ parents (Ryan, 2010a, 2010b), and issues that surface regarding preservice teachers' religious beliefs when it comes to LGBTQ-inclusive texts and teaching (Hermann-Wilmarth, 2008; Hermann-Wilmarth, 2010). These studies have given us an opportunity to see which books work for which students in which grades, how these methods can be incorporated into classrooms with different amounts of curricular freedom, and what kinds of student response to LGBTQ-inclusive lessons result. We've also had the opportunity to write with teachers we've worked with to help them share their ideas and perspectives (Hermann-Wilmarth, Lannen, & Ryan, 2017; Ryan, Patraw, & Bednar, 2013). You'll hear about many of these teachers and classrooms in the pages ahead.

In addition to our identities as White, middle-class, cisgender women—our gender identities align with the sex we were assigned at birth—we also both identify as queer and lesbian. We are privileged to have jobs where we have not been fired for claiming that identity publicly—a privilege that many elementary school teachers who might be LGBTQ don't have, and something that teachers who don't claim LGBTQ identities might never think about. While this work relates to our own identities, it is primarily about children and teachers and the ways we can make education more inclusive for more people. Certainly, we do not speak for all LGBTQ people, nor could we even if we tried. However, our own experiences as teachers, professors, a mom with children in school (Jill), and queer women have shaped our desire to help LGBTQ students and their families be seen and valued.

The Classroom Teachers. Maree Bednar is White and identifies as lesbian and cisgender. She has taught elementary school for more than 25 years in two different urban public schools in a large city in the Midwest. Her former school, where she taught 5th grade, was an underresourced city school attended mostly by African American students located in a neighborhood characterized by high rates of poverty. The first LGBTQ-inclusive lesson she ever taught, which we discuss in Chapter 2, took place at this school. Her current school is a K–8 school in the same city. It has a child-centered informal education philosophy where all members of the school are seen as learners and units are integrated across subject areas and the arts. The school admits students from across the district by lottery and has a racially and socioeconomically diverse student population. We will see teaching she did in 3rd through 5th grades at this at this school in Chapters 3, 4, 5, and 6.

Rose Lannen is White and identifies as a straight, cisgender ally to the LGBTQ community. She is a veteran teacher of more than 20 years. For the last 20 years she has taught 1st through 8th grades at a small private school in a small midwestern city. There is some racial diversity at this school, but minimal socioeconomic diversity. We showcase teaching from her multiage 4th/5th–grade classroom at this school in Chapters 3, 4, 5, and 7.

Barbara O'Grady (a pseudonym) is White and also identifies as a straight, cisgender ally to the LGBTQ community. A veteran teacher of 10 years, Barbara teaches in a small midwestern city in a socioeconomically disadvantaged public school where a majority of the students are African American or Latinx. We see her teaching of 2nd-graders in Chapter 3.

The experiences and classroom snapshots we share in this book are not assurances that these teachers have all the answers to teaching successfully in an LGBTQ-inclusive way or know just what they'd do in every circumstance. In fact, the teachers whose classrooms we invite you into throughout this book have felt the tensions, struggles, and worries that many of you might feel. They each approach LGBTQ topics in different ways, with different texts, and with varied outcomes. They know that this teaching takes reflection and involves missteps as well as continued effort, and sometimes leaves them with more questions than answers. They've been there. But, as we'll show, getting started with inclusive teaching, even in small ways, can make a difference for your students.

A Note on Method

We participated as researchers, supporters, and coteachers in Maree, Rose, and Barbara's respective classrooms for multiple years. The relationships we developed with these teachers over time are professional as well as personal; we travel and present together at conferences; we know each other's families. These are teachers we respect, trust, and love, and we hope they feel the same way about us. After all, they have generously trusted us to design curriculum with them and coteach in their classrooms. We were regular fixtures in these three classrooms, visiting anywhere from a few days a month to a few days a week. The data we drew from when writing this book came from our notes, audio recordings of classroom teaching, teacher interviews and planning sessions, student work samples, and communications with teachers between visits. When we were in these classrooms, our roles involved different levels of coteaching, but we were always more actively involved than just "that lady who sits at the back of the room and takes notes." Students greeted us by name, shared comfortably with us, wrote assignments specifically for our review, and once even included us in their end-of-the-year teacher gifting.

It's hard to synthesize all of these experiences. Like all classrooms, the classrooms we write about are rich and complex spaces. So much happens over the course of a single 60- to 90-minute language arts block, let alone over the weeks and months and years of time that we have been privileged to spend with these teachers and their students. Therefore, rather than a running transcript of hours and hours of classroom practice, we highlight instead some of each teacher's LGBTQ-inclusive ELA moments, using these narratives to help illustrate multiple ways into this kind of teaching. The words of teachers and students, both things they wrote and things they said that we recorded and transcribed, have been edited to fit the conventions of standardized English for readability and clarity. All student names are pseudonyms. The possibilities we suggest are supported by a compilation of hours of data across multiple years and multiple classrooms so that readers might find entry points into LGBTQ-inclusive ELA teaching that feel doable.

How to Use This Book

We understand that what works for one teacher might not work for another, so this book provides a variety of possible entry points into LGBTQ-inclusive teaching. Parts I, II, and III each explore a different approach to LGBTQ-inclusive teaching. The first of the two chapters in each part guides you through key theories that support the teaching method before providing examples of teachers utilizing the methods in individual lessons and other small moments. The second chapter in each part shows how the method can be integrated into larger portions of curriculum such as novel studies, anchor lessons, and units. Finally, the Conclusion provides additional resources and support for teachers to use while continuing their own journeys. Spread throughout the chapters are sections that prompt readers to "Stop and Think." Our hope is that these help readers process new information they're learning, translate key ideas from the classroom examples to their own context, plan for instruction they can try in their own teaching, and collect ideas to share with others. To help readers make connections between the teachers we highlight and their own contexts, we will frequently ask readers to turn away from the text and into their classrooms: How are the classroom scenarios we present helping you think about making space for LGBTQ topics? We hope you will share these ideas with your colleagues, either locally or through national organizations related to LGBTQ topics in schools like those we suggest in the Conclusion chapter.

The overlap between ELA curriculum and LGBTQ-inclusive teaching is what this book is about. We believe teachers can take their desires to meet students where they are; build on what students already know; ask students to be engaged, critical thinkers; and respect the range of experiences students might have while simultaneously teaching the skills mandated by their curriculum. This book is intended for those interested in learning *why* it might be important to talk about LGBTQ topics with young children, even if readers come to the text with questions or concerns. It is also for teachers curious about *how* they might do that kind of teaching in ways that are both educationally sound and that work for their particular school and community context. We invite readers to enter this journey wherever they are, doing what they can to create LGBTQ-inclusive classrooms for the benefit of all students.

In this chapter, we have given a rationale for the importance of LGBTQ-inclusive curriculum for children with LGBTQ families, LGBTQ youth, and those who live in a world with LGBTQ people. Furthermore, we explored why the ELA curriculum is particularly ripe for helping teachers and students include LGBTQ topics. In the next chapter, we will outline the first of three approaches to LGBTQ-inclusive literacy curriculum and highlight the work of teachers who use these approaches in their teaching. Before moving on, let's work through a simple stop-and-think assessment: What are you thinking at this point? Where are you beginning this journey?

STOP AND THINK

- How are you feeling about the idea of including LGBTQ topics in any elementary school classroom? What are your hesitations and questions at this point?
- Think about your own classroom or classrooms you are familiar with. Who would feel represented in the books read aloud to the students? What about the books available to students on the shelves of the classroom library? Who might not see themselves there? Do most of the books in the classroom represent characters of a particular race, class, or gender identity/expression? Is there a possibility to be more inclusive of LGBTQ identities?
- What is one new idea you read about that you want to share with a colleague?

Part I

EXPANDING REPRESENTATIONS OF LGBTQ PEOPLE IN ELEMENTARY ENGLISH LANGUAGE ARTS

My Book Report on *In Our Mothers' House*

[Summary:] In the beginning, I was adopted then Will then finally Millie. When we started to grow up we soon realized that everyone wasn't okay with our mothers. At first we couldn't figure out why that was. Because our mothers taught us that it is okay to be different. When Mrs. Lockner finally gives them the reason . . . You'll have to read the book to find out!

If you're studying homophobia then this is a good book for you to read. This story is full of laughs while it is on subject. It really is a true story embracing what life is like today. In my school there is a lot of teasing associated with [being] gay and lesbian. I myself have witnessed name-calling like (please excuse the small amount of profanity) words like "fag" and "that's so gay" and "you're gay." I myself have been called gay more than once. Believe me it does not feel good. In my opinion, it is a good book for [all] ages and is very on the topic of how you shouldn't be afraid to be different. [. . .]

—Harry, 5th-grade student

Here we have a student who has written a book report on *In Our Mother's House* (Polacco, 2009). He has independently read a book, written a summary of it, identified themes, evaluated the author's craft, and made several text-to-self and text-to-world connections that extended the content of the book into his own life. His response here to an LGBTQ-inclusive book sounds a lot like students' responses to many other kinds of books. But Harry—as a child with straight, married parents whose gender identity and expression fit traditional expectations of "boy"—didn't just wake up one day knowing how to talk and write with deep understanding about the content of this book. Neither did his classmates. His response is an example of the kind of thinking and writing the students were able to do *after* their teacher introduced them to LGBTQ topics, guided their thinking, and provided assignments for them to synthesize their knowledge and show what they'd learned. As Harry's writing here shows, it *is* possible for kids to learn about LGBTQ topics in elementary classrooms as part of their ELA curriculum. So what were the instructional experiences that helped Harry and his classmates develop this kind of ability?

For many teachers new to LGBTQ-inclusive teaching, the most difficult part often is figuring out how to start. You might be asking, "Will I read a book? What book should I use? How do I introduce the book? What prereading activities should I engage in? Will it seem unrelated to other lessons? Should I do something else first? How does this really fit into the curriculum?" The questions alone might lead a teacher to put off LGBTQ inclusion for one more day or week or school year. This chapter is about helping you dive in by finding places to expand your teaching to include (more) LGBTQ people and topics.

In this section, we explore one of the many approaches teachers can use to bring LGBTQ topics into their ELA curriculum: expanding representations. By this, we mean ensuring that your ELA curricular materials, including children's literature, depict LGBTQ people and characters. In Chapter 2, we'll explain how students' own families, their everyday talk, and their experiences with media and current events can all serve as natural springboards for incorporating LGBTQ people into your classroom. These examples will give you models of single lessons to try if you are just getting started with this kind of inclusive teaching. In Chapter 3, we'll turn our attention to larger instructional units and look at how a novel study could be developed around an LGBTQ-inclusive book. We'll introduce you to examples of texts, discussion questions, and assignments you could use in your classroom.

For all of these examples, we'll show you how different teachers have put these ideas into practice. Some teachers include a single book in a one-time read-aloud, while others might stretch their instruction into units that span multiple days or weeks. Some teachers include representations of gay or lesbian people only. Others also share representations of transgender or queer people. One method is not necessarily better or worse than others; the key is thinking about how students in your class might benefit from seeing representations of LGBTQ people presented in ways that make sense in your context. Before we visit those teachers and their classrooms, we want to explain why pedagogical choices that expand representations matter so much for students and how changing who is visible in your teaching materials significantly changes the messages you are sending about the identities people are "allowed" to have.

CHAPTER 2

Introducing LGBTQ People Into Your Teaching

Have you ever Googled yourself or looked yourself up in a yearbook or directory? Do you remember that feeling of "Yep, there I am!" when you find your picture or your name? Most of us like finding ourselves in those moments. We usually feel recognized and important. On the other hand, have you ever been in a meeting or training or professional development session that didn't relate to you or what you do in any way, but you still had to sit through it? Do you remember those feelings of frustration, boredom, or resentment? We generally don't like being left out or having to waste our time with things that are clearly geared toward others and not us. In this chapter, we'll explore how the materials you include in your classroom can work the same way: They can give your students powerful positive feelings of being represented and included, but they can also send messages about who doesn't matter and who isn't appropriate.

Take, for example, the situation of Moriah, a 3rd-grader in a public school in the midwestern United States. Moriah was working at her desk when her teacher, Liz Cook, excitedly called her over to a computer that another child was using to search for books. "Moriah, look!" Ms. Liz said. "There's a new Patricia Polacco book out!" The class had already spent time earlier in the year on a Patricia Polacco author study, and she was well loved by the students in Ms. Liz's class. But Ms. Liz had a very specific reason for wanting to share this particular book with Moriah. "And look, Moriah. Read the title: *In Our Mothers' House*!" Moriah's mouth dropped open for a moment before a huge smile spread across her face. "Hey, that looks like Momma Anne and Momma Leigh!" she exclaimed as she pointed to the two short-haired White women pictured on the book cover. Then her finger drifted to the curly haired African American girl hugging one of the women. "And that looks like me!" She beamed.

This moment was special for Moriah because of its rarity. As an adopted child in a multiracial, lesbian-headed family, she was not used to seeing herself or her family represented in books, particularly books in schools (Ryan, 2010a). When she did, it felt good. This moment showed Moriah that straight, monoracial families were not the only ones allowed in the books in her classroom. It also showed her classmates that Moriah is not the only person in the world with two moms. It brought the reality of diverse families to their attention and showed them that Moriah's experience was one she shared with others. In other words, they recognized that she was not alone. The presence of Moriah's family meant LGBTQ people were already part of the life of this classroom, but the representation of a family like theirs in curricular materials validated that presence. Like a drop of food coloring in a glass of water changes its color, bringing LGBTQ identities into a classroom fundamentally changes the context of the classroom by acknowledging the realities of LGBTQ existence. Developing an understanding of the diverse world we live in is important for all students. It is the kind of learning that can happen when a teacher includes a book with LGBTQ characters in her classroom.

Considering the clear benefits of LGBTQ inclusion to students can be a guide when thinking about why and how to include representations of LGBTQ people in your ELA curriculum. We'll start this chapter by explaining more about why representations matter.

WHY REPRESENTATIONS MATTER FOR KIDS

Rudine Sims Bishop (1990), researching the limited number of African American characters in children's literature, recognized how powerful stories could be for helping people learn about themselves and the world around them. She conceptualized books as serving both as *windows* and *mirrors*. "Mirror books," in this theory, are books that reflect readers back to themselves. They are books where readers are able to see something of their identities, cultures, or experiences in a text. Mirror books validate for readers that they are not alone, that their identity or life experience is not strange, that there might be a community of people just like them out there. When readers receive mirrors for parts of themselves, they get the message that they matter because their experiences are worth writing about and are worth being read. "Window books," on the other hand, give readers insight into another person's experience. Rather than show readers more of themselves, these books show the way into other rooms and worlds that readers haven't seen but can learn from nevertheless. They remind students that not everyone is exactly like them, and they help prepare students for the complexity and diversity of the larger world (Tschida, Ryan, & Ticknor, 2014).

What we need to remember as teachers is that all readers deserve a balance of both windows *and* mirrors. It is this balance that helps us feel affirmed while *also* moving beyond our own limited experiences. It helps children recognize they are not alone while at the same time reminding them that they live in a world with other people who are different than they are. Both sides of this equation are important.

Unfortunately, if we don't actively work to set up our classrooms differently, we tend to have students who get lots of mirrors and very few windows, while other students have lots of windows but very few mirrors. If you did a survey of books in the children's room at the public library, your school library, or your classroom library, you will probably discover that the students who *most often* get mirrors of their own life experiences are White, Christian, middle- or upper-middle-class, able-bodied, English-speaking, girlish girls or boyish boys from families with a married mom and dad. Students who meet this profile get occasional windows into the lives of others, often through biographies or historical fiction, but it is their own lives that are most frequently positioned as neutral or normal. Students and readers who are always peering into the windows of their White, middle-class, cisgender, able-bodied, socioeconomically advantaged peers are rarely offered the experience of being central to a story, which means they don't get to see how people like them navigate the world. Multicultural children's literature matters because it offers possibilities for giving all students more equitable numbers of windows and mirrors. Scholars have shown that children are more engaged when they find themselves somehow in the books or topics addressed in their classrooms (Dutro, 2001, 2009; Emdin, 2016; Enciso, 2004; Harris, 1992; Jones, 2006; Souto-Manning, 2013; Tyson, 1999). When the representations that students see are limited, it has implications for learning. Students get the message that reading and literacy are only for and about certain people, not everyone, and possibly not themselves.

The power of windows and mirrors also applies to representations of LGBTQ identities. Children with LGBTQ parents and family members deserve to see their families in books. Children who might come out later in life deserve to see that LGBTQ characters exist and are worth reading about. Children who don't have a direct connection to LGBTQ people deserve the chance to learn about LGBTQ people in the world.

STOP AND THINK

Consider what representations are already present in your classroom library and curricular materials.

- Do you provide any mirrors for LGBTQ-identified students or students with LGBTQ-identified family members? Do other students have windows into LGBTQ people's lives?
- Who are in the families in the books your students read? Who falls in love in the fairy tales your students study?
- How could those text sets be expanded to include a wider range of human experiences?

DOING THE WORK OF EXPANDING REPRESENTATIONS

There are a variety of options for starting out with this kind of inclusion. Some seem easy to some teachers, but risky to others; different people will find approaches that work best for them and their contexts. For example, if Caitlin heard children telling each other that only boys and girls could get married or that all kids have a mom and a dad, she would gravitate immediately to a read-aloud that children could then talk about. She might choose a book like *Donovan's Big Day* (Newman, 2011) or *And Tango Makes Three* (Richardson & Parnell, 2005) to help start discussions with children about LGBTQ couples and families. Jill, on the other hand, is more likely to begin with a conversation. If she heard students taunting each other on the playground, she might say, "I heard students using words like *faggot* or *queer* to make other students feel bad. Let's talk about what those words mean, and why they might be chosen to hurt people." We might eventually end up having done similar things—Caitlin facilitating a discussion and Jill reading a book—but our entry points would be different. In either situation, though, by including LGBTQ people and ideas, whether through initial read-alouds *or* initial discussions that name identities in elementary school classrooms, teachers supply students with new windows and mirrors of the world around them. Even small efforts in this direction can make a big difference in the lives of students and help change the context of who belongs in schools.

Finding Entry Points to Help You Get Started

So how does teaching in ways that provide additional LGBTQ windows and mirrors actually work? For teachers who are feeling unsure about how to start, we recommend connecting your teaching to situations in your own classrooms and the world in which your students live. This helps you to build on words and ideas that your students already know. While some people worry about forcing an "agenda" of ideas into the classroom that otherwise wouldn't be there, gender and sexuality are already a part of the lives of elementary-school-age students. For example, some students in your class or school may have two moms or two dads or a relative who is transgender. If you spend time in the cafeteria or playground, you'll probably see students play chase-and-kiss games or hear someone get teased for having a crush on someone. Students might talk about certain colors or toys as being "for" certain people. Insults might involve certain slurs that put LGBTQ people down. GLSEN and Harris Interactive (2012) found that 23% of elementary school students reported that not conforming to gender norms was a reason students were bullied, while 21% reported that "acting gay" resulted in bullying from other students. So even if we, as adults, don't catch all these connections to LGBTQ topics, our students are hearing them. Therefore, finding these opportunities to engage requires teachers to listen carefully and know their students and their families.

Three kinds of entry points teachers might consider are (1) connecting to the diverse families in your classroom and school, (2) responding to instances of bullying around LGBTQ identities in your own school, and (3) discussing LGBTQ-related current events. All three of these approaches provide opportunities to include representations of LGBTQ people as a part of ELA curriculum. Like Caitlin and Jill's different approaches to teaching, all of these might start differently, but have similar elements. Our goal is to both demystify the process and help teachers get started.

Connecting to Family Diversity: Seeing It in Practice. In a 1st-grade classroom in a small city in the southeastern United States at a Title I school where over 70% of students qualified for free or reduced-price lunch, Mariana Souto-Manning (Souto-Manning & Hermann-Wilmarth, 2008) learned that Jackson, one of her students, was being made fun of on the playground because he had two moms. The class was just about to start an inquiry project around what makes a family, so Mariana decided she needed to include diverse families in very intentional ways to help address this teasing. To be sure Jackson's family was represented in the unit, she began by searching for texts about gay- and lesbian-headed families to read to her students. She chose to read *Is Your Family Like Mine?* (Abramchik, 1993), a book about a child with two moms. She knew that her students already had language—some of it unkind, some of it personal and about their own lives—around these types of families that might influence how they would respond to the book. Indeed, students shared many different opinions during their reading and discussion, some that even "indicated clear conflict" (Souto-Manning & Hermann-Wilmarth, 2008, p. 272) with each other and the content of the text:

> *Logan:* I don't like this story.
> [*Mariana*]: Why?
> *Logan:* It's just wrong?
> [*Mariana*]: Wrong?
> *Logan:* Yeah. You know, it is not right to have two moms.
> *Kary:* Everybody has one Mom and one Dad.
> *Derrick:* I only have one Dad.
> *Terrence:* I don't have no Dads or Mommas.
> *Logan:* But having two Moms is just wrong. (p. 272)

This discussion gave Mariana a lot of information to work with as she decided where to take the lesson next. Because she had allowed students to explain their thinking in relation to the text they had read, she heard their variety of life experiences and perspectives. This included Derrick and Terrence's announcements about their own family structures as well as Kary and Logan's ideas about lesbian-headed families being impossible or "wrong." Noticing both the conflict among her students and that Jackson, the student with two moms, did not participate in the discussion, Mariana knew that she could not let the conversation rest. She could have simply said, "We're all different!" or "That's not true!" or "Don't say that, that's not nice!" Instead, her pedagogical beliefs regarding multiple perspectives meant that all students deserved to be heard, but she would not allow one voice that disparaged the lives of others to be the last word on a text. She wanted to make space not only for Jackson, the student with two moms, but also for Derrick and Terrence as well as others who might feel different-ly than Logan and Kary regarding gay and lesbian parents. Relying on her knowledge of the available literature, she made the instructional decision to read an additional text to the class.

She reached for another book she'd checked out from the library. *Who's in a Family?* (Skutch, 1995) portrays multiple kinds of multiculturally con-structed family units including, but not limited to, gay- and lesbian-parent-ed families. The book concludes with spaces that invite children to draw pictures of their own families. After reading this second book to the class, Mariana asked her students to go back to their seats and draw their own families. Because she didn't want Jackson to feel singled out, she also drew her family, which, based on her own cultural background, encompassed extended family members. Included in her drawing were her gay uncles. This way, she ensured that she was including families like hers who defined themselves beyond a nuclear family. It also meant she could include LGBTQ representation in the lesson without relying on Jackson to share if he wasn't comfortable doing so. When students giggled as Mariana described her pic-ture of her uncles, she explained that having people she loved laughed at didn't feel good. By describing her own gay family members, she helped students reconsider LGBTQ-headed families:

> *Kary:* You mean there are really some families who have two dads?
> *[Mariana]:* Or two moms [. . .] And we have to be respectful. Even if we don't agree.
> *Logan:* I think two mommies or two daddies are wrong.
> *[Mariana]:* Even if you think this way, you have to be respectful.
> *Logan:* Why?
> *[Mariana]:* Because you would hurt me very much if you were making fun of my uncles who I love so much.
> *Jackson:* You know I have a mom and a dad. They split. Now I have two moms and a dad. And it makes me angry when you make fun of me. (p. 273)

The class never did come to complete agreement about the rightness or wrongness of having two moms. Really, that was never the point. Teaching about LGBTQ people isn't about making students think a certain way. Instead, expanding representations like Mariana did in this lesson helped her students gain a greater understanding of LGBTQ-headed families as one possible family configuration. Furthermore, by reading and talking and drawing about diverse families, the learning environment of the classroom changed. Once Mariana read about and discussed representations of lesbian-headed families, Jackson was able to stand up for himself and explain how the teasing he'd experienced hurt his feelings. After this conversation, other students were able to offer him their support, such as the student who invited Jackson to play at recess, saying "Come on, it's okay. You have two moms and I have one dad. It's fine" (p. 274), and he found a space for himself in the classroom community. Through this lesson, Mariana was able to model respect for family diversity, including for LGBTQ family members, and could emphasize to Logan why his teasing may be hurtful to his classmates. By expanding representations, she not only included more people in the curriculum, but she also made clear that school is a place for all kinds of families and that there is no single definition of "normal." She also made clear her expectations regarding bullying around LGBTQ family members or people by explaining, "In this class, you can disagree, but you can't disrespect" (p. 273).

It can be frightening to have students, even young students, express ideas and beliefs that are in direct opposition to each other. As teachers, we want students to get along; it can make us nervous to facilitate conversations where that doesn't happen easily. Mariana's approach teaches us that if we hone the ways that we listen, even to conflicting ideas, and see those as moments for further discussion and learning rather than a problem we have to fix, our efforts to expand representations of LGBTQ people in our ELA classrooms can be fruitful for developing students' ELA skills and their critical thinking. Even young students are capable of considering diverse perspectives and reflecting on how their responses impact others in their classroom community. Good teaching can help make this possible.

In Mariana's classroom, the teacher responded to Jackson's immediate need to have a mirror of his own family somewhere in the curriculum, which also provided windows on diverse family structures for the other students. Even Logan gained new perspectives.

Logan: You know, I guess all families are okay.

Kary: You mean, if they don't hurt you.

Derrick: This book is about my family. One Dad. But my Dad doesn't have no roommate.

Logan: I guess some people don't think it is right to split up [divorce]. My Dad split up just like in the story [*Daddy's Roommate*].

Tatiauna: Some people don't [think it's] right that I live with my
   momma and grandma.
Logan: But I love my mom and dad even if they split and even if some
   people think that splitting's wrong. (p. 275)

Responding to your specific students' situations and needs in this way is
a productive and important way to approach LGBTQ-content in ELA classrooms, but, while it might feel more immediate or purposeful to teachers
who are otherwise apprehensive about LGBTQ inclusion in curriculum, it
is not the only reason or way in to this work. In fact, in classrooms where
LGBTQ people and families are not readily apparent, it is equally important for teachers to utilize curriculum to facilitate such learning. A classroom
of all White students, for example, still needs to learn about the experiences
and contributions of people of color. So too should a classroom, even one
that "seems straight," include windows to help all students learn about the
experiences and contributions of LGBTQ people.

Responding to Bullying Around LGBTQ Identities: Seeing It in Practice.
In a 4th/5th-grade English language immersion classroom in Arizona in the
early 2000s, Gloria Kauffmann (Schall & Kauffmann, 2003) noticed that
her students were using "gay" as a put-down on the playground. Together,
she and Schall, a university researcher, decided to include books about gay
and lesbian people in the unit to serve as windows for her students. This
was their first time ever including books with LGBTQ content in the classroom, so they made room for lots of discussion prior to reading. In those
discussions, students shared that their use of LGBTQ-related language in
negative and derogatory ways was common in their interactions with each
other, but that they didn't know what the words "gay" and "lesbian" actually meant. They reported hearing these words as insults from other youth,
but they had no adult sources of information explaining these identities.
They just knew that calling someone "gay" was powerful, negative, and
meant to regulate the behavior of students who didn't fit in. One student explained that "basically anyone who is different is in danger of being called
'gay'" (p. 38). Another student reported, "When you are called names you
think you have to change your behavior and your appearance to stop the
name-calling, like 'fag' and 'gay'" (p. 38). As students reflected on their experiences with this kind of bullying, they were frustrated that adults at the
school didn't do more to help them stop it, and they agreed that this kind of
name-calling should be a topic discussed in school.
   To introduce the students to books with gay and lesbian characters, Gloria read *King and King* (de Haan & Nijland, 2002) aloud to the
whole class. This is a book about a prince who falls in love with another prince rather than a princess. Like in Mariana's (Souto-Manning &

Hermann-Wilmarth, 2008) classroom, student responses to the LGBTQ content varied. As Schall and Kauffmann (2003) report, some were surprised and even upset, but others made important connections to their earlier conversation:

> "Prince?" "Prince!" Students burst out with comments, ranging from a horrified, "That's gross!" and "Oh, my god!" to a more measured, "This relates to what we were talking about." They commented that they knew there would be a catch, but they expected it to be something like the Prince marrying an ugly princess. Talk continued with, "This is very weird," and "Is this a children's book?" "This is what kids outside call gay." (p. 39)

Expanding the representations of LGBTQ people in this classroom from playground slurs to characters in fairy tales in the space of an ELA lesson created space for new learning and connections.

Students in the class had differing opinions about the appropriateness of the topic of gay and lesbian people for kids their age—some didn't think they were "ready," while others shared that they had gay family members, and that this topic was not really a big deal for them. After a discussion of *King and King*, Gloria offered students the opportunity to read other picture books about gay and lesbian people. The teacher allowed students to opt out of this part of the unit (although only 5 of the 29 did), and the others had a morning to read silently through a range of texts while Schall, Kauffmann, and a parent volunteer who also served as a translator for some Spanish-speaking students moved through the classroom and spoke with students individually. After individual reading time, the teacher organized students into student-facilitated literature circle groups where they talked through their thoughts and reactions to the texts.

When they came back together as a full group, the students and teachers discussed larger themes they noticed across the text set. Together, they helped the children make sense of the difference between calling somebody "gay" as a put-down and saying that a person is gay or lesbian as a way of factually describing them, although this idea took a while to work through:

> *Imar:* Well, I think in *Daddy's Roommate* [Willhoite, 1990] the mother, I think, she was a little rude for telling the kid that his father was gay.
> *Mayra:* I don't think it was rude, it was just telling him the truth. And maybe she thought that it was time that he should know the truth. And also in another book that I read, they explained to a little girl what gay meant and I think it's the same as in *Daddy's Roommate*, that they think he should know the truth. (p. 41)

Students also suggested that "it's kind of like the same thing as a girl and a boy liking each other but it's a boy and a boy" and that "it's just a different, a different type of love, that's all" (p. 40).

Students' focus in these discussions was on the relationships represented in the books and their thoughts about those. There was no discussion of sex, which makes sense, as Schall and Kauffmann point out, because the books were not about sex. Students did have a few questions about how two men or two women could have children that the teachers weren't able to address because of district policies about sex education, so they simply said that was something they couldn't answer, and the conversation moved on. But students were much more interested in their teachers sharing clear, accurate information about LGBTQ people with them than they were about sex and reproduction. The children in this classroom wondered "why they weren't told [in school prior to this lesson] about the reality of gays and lesbians" (p. 41). They had information from their own lives, but because much of it was used to put down and demean others, those perceptions and misinformation clouded their understanding of actual LGBTQ people.

Through the expanded representations in these stories, students saw gay- and lesbian-identified people living everyday lives, raising children, and, like straight couples in fairy tales, even falling in love. They were also able to practice a variety of language arts skills. During this one morning's lesson, students responded to texts, clarified previous misunderstandings, learned about multiple meanings of words, practiced using vocabulary in more nuanced ways, crafted arguments by building on the comments of others, and deepened their understanding of the diversity in the world.

This lesson all happened in one morning. The teacher did a read-aloud, led a discussion about students' responses to the book, had students read independently, conferenced with them about their individual responses, allowed them to share their responses with one another, and then closed in a full-class conversation. It was an effective way to expand students' understandings of LGBTQ people while also accomplishing language arts work. However, the researcher and teacher from this classroom concluded from the children's own responses that "we didn't need to approach 'gay and lesbian' as an issue or topic separated from the regular curriculum as we did in this experience" (p. 43). Instead, the students themselves made connections between gay and lesbian topics and themes of family, identity, stereotyping, survival, relationships, a sense of belonging, or discrimination, all while directly building on the very words students had been using themselves on the playground.

Discussing LGBTQ-Related Current Events: Seeing It in Practice. As media of all types begin to devote more attention to LGBTQ lives, children have the opportunity to hear about LGBTQ people and topics in many outlets outside of the school walls. Rarely, however, are these messages formulated for children in language they can understand. Discussing these events in school can give students who have heard these messages a chance to discuss them with both peers and adults in developmentally appropriate ways. At the same time, they also give students who haven't yet consciously noticed these messages a chance to see their relevance to children's worlds. Therefore, stories about LGBTQ people that show up in the news, television, movies, and music can provide another entry into ELA study of LGBTQ topics. For example, students might see coming-out stories in pop culture magazines at the grocery store, gay characters in popular sitcoms, a politician's perspective on the rights of transgender people on a cable news show, wedding announcements of lesbian couples in the newspaper, reports of devastating hate crimes in which LGBTQ people are the victims on the local news, or announcements of gay pride festivities on social media. In any of these situations, teachers can respond to and build on the story or event as a concrete starting point for LGBTQ-inclusive teaching.

Responding to a current event in the news was the way that Maree, one of our focal teachers, first started including discussions of LGBTQ people in her urban, underresourced 5th-grade classroom in a midwestern city. Here is Maree's description of what she did in her own words:

Carl Joseph Walker-Hoover. I first heard his name on the national evening news, April 14, 2009. Carl was an 11-year-old African American boy in the 6th grade in a Springfield, Massachusetts charter school. He was a kid active in his church, who played football and basketball, was a boy scout, and had a great smile. He looked like a "regular kid," like the hundreds of intermediate students I had worked with in majority-Black schools during my teaching career. In his face I also saw the face of my own son, an African American 9-year-old who loves to play basketball, also has a great smile, and for whom I have big hopes and dreams. I could not imagine seeing my son's face on the evening news in a story like this.

Carl Joseph Walker-Hoover had been ruthlessly bullied, at school, by kids who repeatedly called him "gay," "girlie," "fag," and other derogatory words often used to target LGBTQ people or those perceived to be LGBTQ. This happened to Carl on a daily basis. Those who targeted him made fun of his clothing, threatened to do him bodily harm, and called him names, all in an effort to hurt and humiliate Carl. His mother, Sirdean Walker, appealed to his teachers and the school officials to intervene on her son's behalf. She tried for much of the school year but the harassment continued until, on April 9, 2009, Carl took his own life. He hanged himself with an extension cord while his mother was downstairs fixing dinner. Ms. Walker found her son a short while later.

I was stunned when I saw the story on the news. It was unbelievable to me that an 11-year-old child could feel so desperate and demoralized that he chose to end his life in order to end the abuse he was suffering. What if this was my son? What about the kids who drove this 11-year-old to his point of desperation? Did they understand the role they played in his death? These are many of the questions I asked while trying to make some sense of this horrific event.

At the time of Carl's death, I was an 18-year veteran teacher assigned to a city school attended mostly by African American students, many of whom were frustratingly designated "low achievers" based on scores from standardized tests. The school was located in an area of our city characterized by high poverty, high crime, and high mobility. The school had been reconstituted, after many years of low test scores, and I was assigned as one of the new staff members expected to turn things around. As a veteran teacher and a lesbian, I was out in my personal life but mostly closeted in my professional life. I had been keeping a low profile at this new school. But that began to change after I learned about the death of Carl Joseph Walker-Hoover.

His death was a pivotal event in my growth as a teacher and activist. It unsettled me in a way I hadn't felt before. As I considered the implications of the death of Carl in the lives of my students, my children, and me, I also began to notice how often I heard the words *fag* and *gay* used at school to hurt and humiliate others. I also realized that I ignored or overlooked these verbal assaults; it was easier not to confront students who shot those poisoned arrows than to have them aimed at me. In my silence, I gave permission, approval, and encouragement for hateful, hurtful words and behaviors in the classroom. Was I any different than the teachers and school officials who looked the other way and, therefore, were complicit in Carl's torment and abuse? My silence was their silence and their silence was deadly. I knew it was time for me to take some action.

I decided to introduce my students to what had happened. Projecting a picture on the overhead projector of Carl in his football uniform, wearing a big smile on his face, I said, "Take a good long look at this face. What are your first impressions of the kid looking back at you? What do you think he's like? Does he look like someone you would like to be friends with?" Students responded with statements like:

"He looks like he's nice."

"He looks happy."

"He looks like a good athlete."

"He looks like he'd be a good friend."

I could tell from their words and the tone in which they spoke that this was a kid they could imagine being friends with, someone who looked like them, their neighbors, and their classmates. I wanted the students to identify with Carl, on some level, before I told them the story of his untimely death.

Then, I explained the situation. "This is a picture of 11-year-old Carl Joseph Walker-Hoover. He was a 6th-grade student in Springfield, Massachusetts. Something really bad happened to him and I want us to talk about it and hopefully learn from his experience. Has anyone seen him in the news or heard about his story?"

Thus began the very first discussion I ever had around LGBTQ topics in my classroom. When I told the students about the bullying Carl endured because his classmates perceived him as gay, and his eventual suicide, their reactions, though varied, were generally strong and full of outrage.

"Why would he kill himself, just because somebody said those things about him?"

"That isn't right!"

"What if he had been gay?" I asked. "Did he deserve to die because of it?"

The students agreed that he didn't deserve to die, even if he had been gay, and that the school should have helped him when he needed it. The more we talked, the more students opened up about their own experiences with LGBTQ people in their families and the community. There was also some whispering and snickering in the room, probably stemming from discomfort, but, by and large, the students showed compassion, empathy, and downright indignation that Carl Joseph Walker-Hoover was bullied to death.

That 40-minute classroom discussion was an eye-opener for me. I realized that I had previously assumed my students knew nothing about LGBTQ people and the issues they face in a world that doesn't accept them, but I was properly put in my place. They had neighbors and family and friends who were connected to the LGBTQ community, in different ways, and they willingly and openly shared their experiences when given the opportunity and encouragement to do so. A door was opened for further discussions to take place about homophobia and the impact it has on all our lives. At the time, in this first discussion, I didn't use the word homophobia. Today, many LGBTQ-inclusive discussions later, I do.

While this lesson might seem like a very small step, it was huge for me and my students. Plain and simple, I learned that elementary students can discuss big topics of relevance to their lives at home, school, and in the community. They are far more insightful than many adults (myself included) give them credit for. They can reflect, see perspectives beyond their own, and develop compassion and caring in the face of injustice. These are attributes of good citizenship necessary for creating communities where all are welcome, valued, and included.

Maree came to LGBTQ-inclusive teaching as an admired and respected teacher, but also as a teacher who had carefully avoided being fully herself in the classroom. As a lesbian, a mother, and a teacher, she saw the tragedy that ended Carl Joseph Walker-Hoover's life as something that deserved a response. She saw how a discussion of this child's life could provide both windows and mirrors for her students. In this way, she expanded the representations of who they might understand to be a part of the LGBTQ community, and showed them that ELA time was an appropriate time in which to learn about the world around them.

This ELA lesson did not revolve around a children's literature text; nevertheless, it fostered many ELA skills, particularly ones around speaking, listening, and viewing visual representations. In only 40 minutes, Maree challenged students to make text-to-world connections between a current event and their own lives. She also fostered students' discussion skills and the critical thinking required for students to explain their thinking and give evidence for their positions. By using an image rather than a book, Maree helped students notice the power of meaning-making that occurs at a glance, and she laid the groundwork for students' future visual literacy skills.

The main idea here is for teachers to talk with their classroom communities about LGBTQ-related stories just as they would about other events in the world that their students have questions about or that they want to help their students understand. In other words, instead of self-censoring LGBTQ-related stories in the news, we hope you will see these as an opportunity to build on topics that students are hearing about but may not fully understand. Just as children's literature can provide an entry point for teaching, discussions of current events can work in the same way, particularly if you already include current events as a regular part of your classroom practice. So, if you are a teacher who teaches with Scholastic News or asks students to bring in newspaper articles to discuss or if you already connect curricular ideas in math (to local businesses) or social studies (to current elections) or science (to the local weather), then connecting current events regarding LGBTQ people or topics can be an ideal fit. When examining current events are a common pedagogical practice, news stories are a part of classroom talk, so if students bring up LGBTQ-inclusive stories, having tools for leading these conversations can help teachers. When expanding representations through current events, teachers can use local, state, or national events to ask, "Did you know this was going on in the city/state/world? What do we know about this event? How are LGBTQ people a part of this event? What are the effects of this event? Who is or will be most affected? In what ways? How is this similar to other things we've read or studied?"

Finding Familiar ELA Practices in This New Teaching

These three lessons, taught by different teachers, across different grade levels, in different parts of the country, and spread throughout different years, were all ELA lessons. They all engaged students in developing their abilities in the interconnected areas of reading, writing, speaking, listening, viewing, and visually representing. They also all included representations of LGBTQ people, thereby expanding the windows and mirrors available to students. For these teachers, ELA instruction was a way to explore perspectives and a chance to learn more about the diversity in their classroom and beyond. Each discussion took up only a small amount of instructional time in the respective classroom, yet helped students develop skills of lifelong readers, writers, and thinkers.

Specifically, these teachers turned to several familiar practices to accomplish these goals. Mariana and Gloria used developmentally appropriate children's literature titles while Maree employed other text formats like pictures and the nightly news. They all engaged in prereading discussions to assess and activate background knowledge. They allowed students to respond to the texts they shared in authentic ways that gave students a chance to voice and visualize their thoughts in multiple settings and formats. They varied their instruction between full-class, small-group, and independent work formats. They helped students learn new meanings of familiar words. They allowed students to compare what they read to other books in similar genres. They led discussions that helped students focus on larger themes like acceptance and community. They engaged in formative assessment of student understanding through class discussions, one-on-one conferences, and student work products.

But perhaps most importantly, these three teachers encouraged students in their classes to turn to texts as a tool to better understand their own lives and situations that they either participated in or observed at school. Seeing LGBTQ characters cast in familiar genres helped students increase their understanding of LGBTQ people's lives. Students were asked to learn about, often for the first time in school, how LGBTQ people live, build families, and, sometimes, experience bullying and harassment. They got to ask questions about these ideas and share the connections they had. They saw that LGBTQ people were not separate and apart from the rest of the curriculum they were immersed in just as they are not separate and apart from their experiences in the larger world. Reading about these situations on the page brought new awareness and understanding to real people in their own lives and larger communities. Students connected with classmates who had been left out, asked questions they hadn't previously had the chance to ask, and learned compassion for those in their communities who were being mistreated. This helped build students into more responsive citizens and more sensitive neighbors. These approaches to text are at the fingertips of many ELA teachers, making them accessible entry points for expanding representations of LGBTQ people in elementary classrooms.

STOP AND THINK

- What are some of the ELA practices you recognized in these lessons?
- What other practices are you most comfortable with or do you find most effective?
- Are there any of those that you feel you could use to expand representations of LGBTQ people in your own teaching?

CONSIDERATIONS AND CHALLENGES IN YOUR CONTEXT

This chapter has laid out ways that teachers can expand the representations in their classrooms to include LGBTQ lives. At the same time, we also acknowledge that this approach to addressing LGBTQ topics in elementary ELA classrooms comes with some challenges for teachers in certain contexts. This approach, because it involves explicit teaching about LGBTQ people and characters, could lead to objections from parents or administrators who do not want LGBTQ-inclusive materials to be shared with children. This kind of backlash could, in some cases, threaten teachers' professional standing or even their job security. This is a particular risk for new teachers and for those without employment protections. We offer a different, less direct approach to LGBTQ-inclusive teaching in Part II, and we talk more about how to mitigate risks and backlash in the Conclusion, both of which might be helpful for those in more challenging contexts, but we also find it instructive to look at what the teachers portrayed here did to deal with their own, similar risks.

For some teachers, a general conversation about the overall topics you'll be teaching can help people understand your plans and can divert possible tension. Mariana Souto-Manning (Souto-Manning & Hermann-Wilmarth, 2008), for example, wished that she had alerted the parents of her students that the class would be reading about families that might be different from their own. Because of the range of diversity—visible or not—in all classrooms, this approach lets parents know that their children's ideas about what is "normal" (i.e., their own lives) will be challenged, but that this expansion of ideas is a regular part of deep classroom inquiry. When Mariana did have a few parents object to her lesson, claiming that her inclusion of gay and lesbian families in a 1st-grade classroom was inappropriate, she was able to explain how the read-aloud and related activities happened in response to student comments and within the classroom study of family.

Gloria Kauffmann (Schall & Kauffmann, 2003) gave students in her upper elementary class the choice to participate in lessons where they read books with LGBTQ characters. The few students who opted out by their own choice participated in ELA activities that were related but did not contain LGBTQ content. By giving students agency and not requiring participation, Kauffmann felt protected from parental and administrative criticism. Likewise, by continuing to offer LGBTQ content to the rest of the class, she emphasized the importance of these conversations. She made accommodations for students who needed them, but also went ahead with her plans for more inclusive teaching.

Maree had resisted including LGBTQ content in her teaching—including outing herself and intervening in LGBTQ-related bullying—because she was worried about her own safety as an LGBTQ person as well as the resistance that she might face in the community in which she was teaching. When, after the death of a child, she was moved beyond these concerns, she learned through her brave inclusion of LGBTQ people in her classroom that her worry was largely unfounded. The discussion, teaching, and learning went over just like any other discussion, teaching, and learning—ultimately, it involved some resistance, some more and some less active participation, and different kinds of growth for each student. By taking a chance that she had previously been too nervous to take, she learned that elementary ELA is, in fact, a place where expanding representations of LGBTQ people is both possible and important.

There are a few other possible challenges to teaching about LGBTQ people through expanding representations that teachers should consider. For example, sometimes reading a single book with LGBTQ characters can further tokenize these identities (Clark & Blackburn, 2009), much like making a point of reading books with African American characters only in February during celebrations of Black History Month relegates an entire population to one month of the year. While reading even one mirror book can be powerful for a child that needs it, teachers might be tempted to feel like reading an LGBTQ-inclusive book in a single lesson helps them check off something that they are done with rather than starting a larger journey of LGBTQ-inclusive teaching. Additionally, the representations offered by easily accessible children's literature are limited. While the number and quality of LGBTQ-inclusive books for elementary-school-age readers continues to grow, there are still not many, they may not always be easy to find, and those that exist often fail to include diverse representations (Hermann-Wilmarth & Ryan, 2016). For example, what about LGBTQ people who are not White or suburban? Or LGBTQ parents who are not partnered? This lack of diversity will be addressed more fully in Chapters 6 and 7, but it is important to remember that teachers cannot count on a book or two to provide a window (or a mirror) into the full range of LGBTQ lives. Not every lesson can (or should) be expected to take on all of these considerations, but they are important to keep in mind over the days and weeks and years of a teacher's practice to be sure that inclusive teaching is truly inclusive.

Nevertheless, even a single representation, shared respectfully, can provide a new window or mirror in a way that makes a difference for children. We believe that the approaches taken by the teachers in this chapter—choosing texts thoughtfully, responding to situations in the classroom and the larger world, and inviting students' reflections and connections—can all help to harness the power of LGBTQ-inclusive texts within specific contexts. We will explore further in Part II how it is possible to use "straight" texts that help to trouble taken-for-granted notions regarding gender and sexuality.

CHAPTER 3

Expanding LGBTQ Representations Through Novel Studies

Paul: Can I ask a question?
Maree: Sure.
Paul: Can we read some more?
Maree: What do you think? Should we read a little bit more?
Students: YES!!!!

—Maree, talking and reading with her 4th-graders

There is a buzz of energy on the read-aloud carpet in Maree's 4th-grade classroom. She's reading James Howe's (2005) *Totally Joe* with her class, and the students are deeply engaged. When the protagonist, a 7th-grader named Joe, says "drumroll please," the 4th-graders start to drum on the floor or their legs as they sit on the read-aloud carpet. When Joe throws a taunt back at his bully, a group of boys in the front of the room exclaim "Ouch!" Another says triumphantly, "Ooooh, you got served!" And when Joe finally declares, "Colin Briggs is my boyfriend," the children gleefully squeal and giggle as one girl says, "I knew it!" Their expressive engagements (Sipe, 2002) show that not only are they listening and comprehending this book, but they are actively participating, enjoying, and making the story their own.

A few states away, a similar kind of enthusiasm can also be found in Rose's 4th- and 5th-grade classroom. With her finger between the first two chapters, Rose pauses in her reading of Alex Gino's (2015) *George*. She leans forward in her chair, getting closer to her students who are sitting on low benches around a carpet in the class's meeting area. Their eyes are on her, waiting. Rose asks, slowly, "So, what do you think about George?" Among the shuffling and din of voices, Jonas comments, "Either George is a girl with a boy name or . . . " When he trails off in an uncertain tone without finishing his sentence, Rose interjects, "Ahh. You noticed different pronouns: 'she' and 'bro.'" Alice, who had already read this book independently, added, "Can I just say what the pronoun thing is? So, George

37

was born as a male but, um, she believes that she is a girl. And um, and she's hiding it." Rose nods and Peter adds, "So, George could be a boy name or a girl name because it could be like, Georgette." "Maybe," Rose answers. "What about you, Camilla?" "Well, maybe, like Alice said, in part of her life, she might, like, become a female?" Grinning, Rose asks, "Should we read and find out?" The collective "YES" from students inspires her to adjust her glasses and open to the second chapter.

Even when teachers might feel okay including a book with two moms in a unit on families or putting other LGBTQ-inclusive books on their shelves for students to choose on their own, they often still express discomfort about planning a full unit of study or other extended learning around LGBTQ-inclusive books. You might be one of those teachers; we certainly used to be. Teachers we've talked to worry about the books being appropriate for their students. They worry about how kids will react or if they'll be able to connect to the story. They worry about being able to answer students' questions. And they worry about what their students' parents and their administrators will think. Those worries might increase when it comes to books that feature LGBTQ protagonists rather than LGBTQ-headed families, especially if those protagonists are youth. Those are all worthwhile concerns to think through, and you can read more about facing parental and administrative concerns in the Conclusion. But after participating in classrooms where students read LGBTQ-inclusive novels as a class, we know that the benefits related to student learning and engagement are worth it. Not only can students in elementary schools "handle" books with LGBTQ characters, they can engage with, learn from, and even love them, just like they did in Rose's and Maree's classrooms. We believe that not only can teachers and administrators see these benefits, but parents, when walked through the rationale, often see them, too.

In the previous chapter, we saw ways teachers took advantage of small moments and individual lessons in their ELA teaching to include representations of LGBTQ people. In this chapter, we will present strategies to integrate LGBTQ-inclusive teaching into ELA curriculum in more substantial ways. To do this, we'll take a longer, deeper look at Rose's private 4th/5th-grade class and Maree's public 4th-grade class to see what elementary ELA teaching can look like when books including LGBTQ characters become the basis for an entire unit or novel study. Using moments from their classrooms, we will describe how this kind of teaching plays out in real-life situations, including books read, discussion questions asked, writing prompts assigned, and responses children had to these topics. We will also show how Rose and Maree attended in very concrete ways to the teaching of ELA, including their instruction related to oral language, letter writing, point of view, character traits, inferential thinking, intertextual connections, the use of textual evidence, and vocabulary, among other practices. In other words, the skills that many teachers emphasize in their ELA instruction and novel studies generally can also be addressed when the novel happens to include an LGBTQ character that expands the available representations in their classrooms.

We want to note for readers that while both Rose and Maree are experienced teachers who previously found smaller ways to weave LGBTQ identities into their classroom instruction, neither of them had experience with putting these identities at the center of their teaching over a longer time period. Therefore, the stories here show you these teachers' early attempts at this kind of instruction. What they and their students do and say isn't always perfect and polished, but it's most certainly real. We hope that seeing teachers work their way through their first tries at extended LGBTQ-inclusive instruction will demonstrate the incredibly powerful moments that can happen when we engage students in deep thinking about high-quality books whose messages help students learn about and make a difference in the world.

TEACHING A NOVEL WITH A GAY PROTAGONIST

The year that Maree first taught the novel *Totally Joe* (Howe, 2005), she was teaching a 4th-grade class of 29 students, diverse in terms of race, class, religion, abilities, and family structures. Following the practices of their school's informal education philosophy, Maree and her teaching partner had decided on an overarching inquiry question of "What Does It Mean to be a Problem Solver" that would guide their work across all subject areas for the year. In addition to doing guided reading with primarily nonfiction texts, Maree used her ELA time to read a wide variety of books to and with her students that brought up social issues and highlighted ways children could be problem solvers in those situations. They started with *Maniac Magee* (Spinelli, 1990) then moved through other novels including *Esperanza Rising* (Ryan, 2000), *Crooked River* (Pearsall, 2005), *Number the Stars* (Lowry, 1989), *A Friendship For Today* (McKissack, 2007), and *The Giver* (Lowry, 1993). With each of these novels, Maree led students in extensive conversations about the social issues, themes, and main ideas of these texts. This helped her students build an understanding of racism, classism, xenophobia, anti-Semitism, ageism, and other kinds of marginalization around difference, which the class eventually came to call "the -isms." At the same time, she used these novel studies to help students learn skills like story elements, character analysis, cause and effect, problem and solution, main idea and supporting details, and author's problem and purpose.

It was after reflecting on where she next wanted to take the conversations about prejudice, difference, and problem solving that her students had been having that Maree decided to include a novel featuring an openly gay protagonist, Joe of *Totally Joe*. She found Joe to be a funny and relatable character and she thought the "alphabiography" structure of the text—an autobiography with a chapter for each letter of the alphabet, following an "A is for. . . . B is for . . ." structure—would be entertaining for her students. She also liked how even though Joe was a bit older than her students, his sense of romance and physical affection was in keeping with most of her own students' developmental level in that he was interested in having a boyfriend and holding hands but didn't feel like kissing anyone yet. Chapter 11 in the book is actually called "K is *Not* for Kissing" and when he talks about kissing, he apologizes to his teacher "for having to get all R-rated" (p. 89). In this next section, we will highlight how Maree structured and conducted this novel study and the ways students responded to give you concrete ideas on how to get started in your own classroom.

Beginning to Teach *Totally Joe*

Like she did with many read-alouds, a few days before Maree began *Totally Joe* she told her students it was the book they would read next. She showed them the cover, read a few lines from the back of the book, and left it on the chalk tray where she often displayed books. A few students investigated it further, but most did not. On the day Maree began reading, she introduced the text by talking about other books that the author, James Howe, had written. By connecting to other books her students had read, she positioned *Totally Joe* as just another book in their curriculum rather than as unique or strange because of its content. She said, "We're going to be starting a new book called *Totally Joe*. *Totally Joe* is by James Howe. Put your hand in the air if you've ever read *Bunnicula*." Students' hands shot up and there were lots of "ooh!"s and "I love *Bunnicula*"s whispered. Maree continued, "I bet you have read other books by James Howe . . ." As she read out various titles listed on the back cover, students grew increasingly excited.

Maree's next decision was to continue her introduction of the book by reading directly from the summary of the text on the back cover. This way, she drew on the work the publisher had already done to make the book interesting and accessible; she didn't have to come up with exactly what to say on her own. This strategy provided her with a surer footing. This summary introduced the students to some initial ideas about the character and the structure of the text, including mentioning how Colin is Joe's "secret boyfriend" and that the story is "an exuberant, funny, totally original story of one boy's coming out and coming of age." Just as it was meant to, this blurb activated students' curiosity and interest.

Finally, after reading the summary, Maree asked the class "How many of you really like who you are?" This big, open-ended question required students to reflect on their own experiences related to an idea they'd just heard about. In this way, Maree was already helping students think about a key theme in the text and the ways that theme might be meaningful to their own lives. After students responded with nods and raised hands, Maree continued, emphasizing how this theme is important both for Joe and for them, saying, "Something that I really like about this character is that he's okay with [being himself] because he *likes* who he is. And that's so important to our self-esteem that we like who we are. And though we're all really different, we can like who we are." In this simple statement she affirmed that this character was someone worth liking, connected her students' human experiences with what they were going to be reading about, highlighted the diversity in their class, and emphasized the important role of those individual differences. And with that, she began to read.

How Maree Reads Aloud

Maree's read-alouds, whether or not the book had LGBTQ characters, took on a fairly familiar "before-during-after" structure that was shaped by her ongoing, formative assessment of students' understanding and areas of confusion.

Before Reading. Most days Maree would begin her ELA time by calling everyone over to the carpet. Then, she did an introduction or recap before reading. This time helped get students thinking about what had been happening in the story to this point and any big ideas she wanted them to reflect on. It also helped catch up any students who might have been absent the day before. Moreover, recapping as an introduction to the day's reading gave Maree an opportunity to highlight key ideas from the previous chapter that students had had time to think about and allowed her to connect these discussions to background knowledge they had built earlier in their reading or while reading other books. This scaffolded students' use of that knowledge in their own talk. As a result of these connections and her openness to students sharing their own perspectives, some of the students' most sophisticated thinking happened during these times.

This process of review-and-discuss to build background knowledge was how Maree started the second day of her *Totally Joe* read-aloud. She reminded the students that they had ended the day before with reading the first page of the chapter "B is for Boy" and she wanted "to recap" that with them. The resulting conversation focused on how the character Kevin Hennessey had called Joe a "girl" in gym class, and included a quick exploration of some of the most common stereotypes for boys and girls because "we have certain stereotypes about what a boy is and what a girl is." This conversation allowed a discussion of these ideas as well as a review of some key terminology. For example, when one student shared a stereotype about girls, another student questioned, "Is that true?" The student responded, "It's a *stereotype*." Here, Maree was able to follow up with additional clarification about how a stereotype is an idea that "our culture in general . . . as a whole" tends to hold. Listening to her students' ideas let her know what information they were understanding and what support they still needed. Maree wrapped up this discussion by reminding students to keep the words for these stereotypes and their own lived experiences in mind as they read this book. This prereading work, therefore, better prepared them to read the "B is for Boy" chapter about name-calling and gender stereotypes.

During Reading. As Maree read aloud to students, she used vocal inflection and expression to create engagement, illustrate character traits, and highlight the meaning of the text. In this way, her voice and her reading became a key scaffold for student enjoyment and understanding. She would sometimes read many pages at a time without interruption so students could hear, enjoy, and think about the story. When she paused, it was usually to model her thinking, ask students for their thoughts, or to take student questions.

Often, these stopping points helped students understand and generalize the themes of the text to their own lives. Here's a discussion Maree and her students had during the "C is for Colin" chapter:

Maree: What do you think [Colin] might have meant by that, "I wish I could be like you?" What's a possibility? Megan?

Megan: Not caring about what other people think about you.

Brittney: I wish. . . . I don't want to say . . . well maybe he's saying I don't want to be like any other people, I want to be like you.

Maree: How many of you . . . you don't have to put your hand up, but think about this for a second . . . do you think as much as we want to be who we are, that we do feel pressure from other people to be who they think we should be, or do you ever feel pressure to be a certain way because you're a girl or a boy or you're Black or you're White or something like that? How many of you have felt some kind of pressure to be a certain way because of your gender, your race, your religion, or anything about you? I certainly have, I know. And some of you have, yeah. Some of you have. And let me ask you this follow-up question: Is it hard to pretend to be somebody you're not or try to live a certain way when it doesn't fit for you? How many of you think that's really, really hard? Without telling me the specific situation, I wonder if anyone would be willing to share why that is hard or what is hard about it. Without really telling us what the situation is. What's hard about it?

Ashley: It's hard because . . . it just kind of feels uncomfortable sometimes because it's like when, for example, if you like sit in a different spot or if you do really anything different it feels different . . . so it's uncomfortable and it's hard because . . . you can't really change that because you're you.

Indira: It might be some habits you have. Like if it's what you're used to, like if you see a ball and you want to go kick it because that's what you're used to . . . like you're not supposed to chew your nails.

Zuzy: It's like Indira said about trying to break a bad habit . . . it's really hard and it doesn't feel right.

Maree: I keep coming back to that idea of discomfort, it feels uncomfortable. Okay, let's read on.

At other times, Maree's stopping points helped her uncover students' multiple perspectives on a topic, especially when they involved life experiences that might be unfamiliar to them. Here's a conversation they had during Maree's reading of the "D is for Dating" chapter:

Maree: Can I ask you guys a question? Let me reread a portion here. "It's just that I want people to think Colin and I are cute too and I want to hold hands in the hall." What does he really want?

Ashley: I think what he really wants is people to notice that he and Colin are together but not tease them about it. He wants them to accept that Colin and him are dating.

Arnold: He wants people to accept him just for who he is and for the fact that he likes other boys.

Maree: Anyone else?

Violet: He doesn't like to have to keep secret so people won't bully him.

Charlotte: He wants people to think that gay people are okay, like they aren't that much different and they aren't bad.

In these discussions, Maree helps students connect directly to the text by asking them to share their own experiences and make inferences about ideas in the text that weren't explicitly stated. As she helps students connect to Joe, she reminds them that they each are unique, while still drawing their attention to their many shared experiences. Using text-to-self connections and the words of the book directly, Maree invites students to create empathy for characters they have just met.

After Reading. After reading a section or chapter, Maree would usually engage students in reflection again. Sometimes this would take place through discussion. Other times it would be an idea that she wanted students to reflect on independently, often using the results of that thinking to start the next day's reading time. With *Totally Joe*, this "after reading" reflection was easy to do because each chapter ended with a "life lesson" that communicated a key idea about the text. This helped Maree scaffold their understanding of major textual themes within and across texts. For example, after the first chapter of *Totally Joe*, Maree helped students see how discussions of difference they'd had across many of their previous read-alouds were also showing up in this text. She asked what the life lesson "when you're a boy like me you kinda get noticed all the time" really meant. Alianna said, "I'm guessing it means if you're different . . . and if you're different in what everybody thinks is a bad way . . . then you kinda get picked on and talked about all the time." Maree replied, "Here's that theme of difference . . . again. It seems to come up in all these books we're reading. The whole idea of different being what? Different being . . . bad. Yeah. Here we go again guys, wow." In this way, she was able to close her reading time with a reinforcement of themes that had structured their whole semester and were supporting their understanding of this LGBTQ-inclusive text.

Saying "Gay" in the Classroom

When Maree read *Totally Joe*, she made pedagogical choices that helped students explore LGBTQ topics in and related to the text. Sometimes these involved helping students connect their own lives to big ideas in the story, demonstrating the overarching human connections between them and this gay protagonist. But other times she directed their attention to the LGBTQ-specific information in the text through more explicit prompting. Such additional scaffolding was necessary because these terms and ideas were new to some students, but also because none of the students had had much previous experience discussing LGBTQ topics in school.

After her reading of the first chapter, "A is for Addie," for example, Maree prompted students with a series of direct questions to establish the terms "gay," "ally," and "bully." For example, Maree asked the students, "What do you think Joe's difference is in this book? What, uh, we haven't heard it . . . he has not come out and said anything. So . . . what do you think the difference is, his difference? That he's what?" After this prompting,

Kayla quickly said, "He's gay." Maree responded, "That he's gay? How many of you think that Joe's probably gay?" Many students raised their hands. Once this had been established, Maree returned to Joe's description of Addie and how she had "always stood up for" him. Maree asked, "What would we call a person like Addie who stands by him all the time? Someone in his life who always stands up for him?" One student suggested "friend," but another student said "ally." Maree agreed and explained that an ally "stands up for him when people are mistreating him," which is something important for "a kid like Joe" to have. And finally, she said, "Now Kevin Hennesy, who makes fun of [Joe] and trips him and pulls his hair, all of those things. What would we call someone like Kevin?" When students answered, "a bully," Maree agreed.

Sometimes this more direct support related to LGBTQ topics grew from students' own reactions and responses, like the first time the slur "faggot" was used in the book. In the "B is for Boy" chapter, Maree read, "Today in gym Kevin Hennessy called me a girl. I reminded him that we were trying to stop name-calling in our school. He said, "I'm not calling you a name, faggot. I'm calling you a girl, which you are.'" The students immediately erupted in discussion and whispers. When a student said "I've never even heard that word before," Maree opened up a larger conversation to discuss it:

> *Maree:* Who's never heard that word before? Hands down. Who has heard that word before? Okay. Would somebody who's heard the word before be willing to tell us what that word means as I just read it . . . as I just read it? What do you think? Could you share with us what that word means, how it gets used in our culture? Like if somebody calls you a faggot, what are they saying?
>
> *Paul:* I've been called a faggot.
>
> *James:* Basically, it means like you're gay . . . it's like, it's a really mean way of calling somebody gay.
>
> *Maree:* Yeah. It's a really mean way of calling somebody gay. . . . It's calling somebody gay as a put-down, isn't it?
>
> *James:* Yeah.
>
> *Phil:* I hear people say "You're gay."
>
> *Harry:* The big kids [at school] say it.
>
> *Violet:* Sometimes people in our school, not saying very many people do it, some people use "gay" as like an insult.
>
> *Paul:* Or a put-down.
>
> *Violet:* That's mean.
>
> *Maree:* Yes. Yeah, it is. If someone calls you "gay" as a put-down or calls you "faggot" as a put-down, what is the hidden message? Well, it's not so hidden! What is the non-spoken message in that?
>
> *Brittney:* You're not like, you're not like everyone else, you're your own kind. You're like, not . . . like everyone . . .

Maree: You're not like everyone else . . .

Imani: You're different.

Harry: You're not a human being.

Maree: You're not like a human being. Did you want to say . . .

Paul: Nobody likes you.

Maree: Nobody likes you.

Alianna: You're just NOT. Your being is just NOT.

Maree: You're NOT. Okay. Zuzy?

Zuzy: Like you're gay and it's not a good thing.

Maree: Like it's not a good thing.

Anna: You're different.

Maree: You're different. There's something wrong with you. Do you
hear that message in that?

Alianna: That's so mean.

Maree: Yeah. Like if somebody says, "Hey, faggot." There's something
wrong with you in that person's view. They are insulting you in
what they view to be and what our culture views as one of the
biggest insults you can throw someone's way. Isn't that interesting?

These moments can cause a teacher to second-guess their decision to
include books like *Totally Joe* in their elementary classrooms. It can seem
easier to simply avoid texts that invite this kind of frank discussion. But,
as Maree's students show, we can't ignore these topics when students hear
these words in their everyday lives anyway, sometimes even directed at
them. In this example, instead of glossing over words like *faggot* when they
appeared in the book, Maree followed the author's lead of putting it in the
book in the first place and talked to her students about it. When some students had no familiarity with that particular word, she not only defined it,
but she went further, leading a dialogue with students about how that word
feels and how it positions people.

During that discussion, Maree accepted and validated multiple students'
thoughts, restating each comment to be sure it was heard by the whole
group. Yet she also pushed students to notice the deeper social forces at
play when people are marginalized or put down because of their gender or
sexuality. Certainly, this helped students' comprehension of the text because
they understood that Joe's bully does not believe that Joe is fully human.
But it also deepened students' comprehension of how language works in the
world outside of Joe's story, including at their school. These discussions relied on the vocabulary work the class had been engaged with all year when
discussing other social justice topics—words like *ally*, *difference*, and *bully*
were not new. But with *Totally Joe*, Maree and the students built on those
connections while drilling down into the specifics of the meanings of these
words for the LGBTQ community.

TEACHING A NOVEL WITH A TRANSGENDER PROTAGONIST

The teaching in Rose's 4th/5th-grade class at a private school in a small midwestern city regularly included texts that represented a wide range of identity categories and experiences. Over the first half of this particular school year, Rose and Jill had cotaught an ELA curriculum that investigated a variety of social justice–related topics including Japanese internment camps, the removal of the Confederate flag from the state house in South Carolina, and the lack of representation of African Americans in texts about American history. Rose had not, however, taught a novel with a transgender protagonist like in Gino's (2015) *George*. She reported feeling trepidation about reading *George* with this particular class because her focus on social justice as a yearlong theme had caused concern for one parent. But Rose was committed to representing transgender identities because they were a part of their school community, including an out (and beloved) transgender teacher. Even more than that, Rose included *George* in her curriculum because, "I want [my students] to be and become people that understand that there are all different ways of being, and . . . this is work that has to keep happening. We can't just say, 'oh, we did that for a semester and we got there. We aren't racist or sexist or homophobic or whatever.'" So, she decided to ask for approval from her Head of School to read the book with her class. When she received that approval, she decided to move ahead with the unit.

In the book, the protagonist knows she is female and calls herself Melissa although she was named George and assigned male at birth. She is referred to as "he" and "George" by all other characters. The reader understands this nuance because the third-person omniscient narrator refers to Melissa with female pronouns, but by the name "George." It isn't until the end of the book, after Melissa has revealed this name to her best friend, that the narrator stops calling her George and starts calling her Melissa. In our writing here and in class discussions, Rose, Jill, and the students followed the narrator's guide, using "she" and "George" until the narrator uses Melissa. When we refer to her as a character, generally, we use Melissa since that's her core identity.

The plot that drives the story involves Melissa's 4th-grade class preparing a performance of *Charlotte's Web*. When George auditions for the role of Charlotte, she is told, to her deep disappointment, that only girls are allowed to try out for girl parts. Her teacher will not bend the rules around gender for anyone, even as George does not see herself as bending the rules since she is a girl. Since her school only knows her as George and has no knowledge of her self-identification as female, they disqualify her, regardless of her preparedness for the part. As the plot progresses, George comes out as a girl to her best friend Kelly, who had won the role of Charlotte in the play. The two friends hatch a plot where Kelly will perform Charlotte in the first performance of the play, and George will put on Kelly's spider costume and perform Charlotte in the second performance.

Procedures and Activities

Just as Maree did, Rose used her everyday read-aloud procedures when reading this book, reading aloud three times a week over the course of a month. She began with students gathered in the class meeting area, where she and Jill would review the plot points from the previous chapter and facilitate discussions around students' responses to short answer questions assigned for homework the previous day. At that point, they would read a new chapter or two, pausing to answer clarifying questions with regard to vocabulary or plot points that might be confusing. After finishing the chapter, they would ask students to discuss initial reactions to what had happened, make predictions about what was to come, and preview that night's homework questions.

Even though this read-aloud structure was something Rose had used before, the transgender content of this text was new. Here, we share two ELA-specific activities that proved particularly helpful in guiding student understanding of both text and content. First, the class had whole-class discussions that led into acting out scenes in the text to help them think through multiple perspectives of what it might be like to be George as her transgender identity was made public. Second, by writing letters to the author of the text, students put their knowledge of the character and transgender topics into a writing project with an authentic audience.

Book Discussions with Dramatic Interpretation. At the climax of the book, after George and Kelly have successfully switched roles in the play, George's mother comes backstage upset and confused, ready to confront George, but Principal Moldanado intervenes, praising George's performance. After reading, Rose asked the students to reflect on these characters' responses, beginning a deep discussion about the reading.

Camilla responded to Rose's inquiry by saying, "I think that George's mom was really surprised and really disappointed, and doesn't really know who George is or understand it. But, I think the principal's reaction was really good, and I think she knew what was going on with George." Rose agreed, "I think so, too. One of the things I noticed while they were talking was that Principal Moldanado never referred to George as "he." Did you notice that, too?" As students nodded and agreed, Rose returned to the text and read the gender-neutral words that the principal used to speak with George's mom: "star," "kid," "actor," "children." This pattern of punctuating discussion with rereading parts of the text to clarify, remind, or correct misconceptions is part and parcel of the reading comprehension teaching that Rose employs. As she was doing this teaching of skills, Rose also invited her students to notice how gender works in the text. By paying attention to the specific words used by the principal, Rose and the students learn about the principal—that she respects and, perhaps, understands who George is—and provides a model for speaking without misgendering people. While the author did the work of providing sample language, Rose made sure to draw attention to it. While students might have noticed the same language while independently reading this book, in this instance, the read-aloud structure made this work seamless.

One worry that many teachers have with regard to LGBTQ topics is what to do when they make a mistake. This happened a bit later in the class discussion when Rose accidently misgendered George. Another student asked about a moment when George saw her bully at the play. Rose said, "Yes, and what did he wonder [when seeing the bully]?" In unison, the class corrected Rose, who had just misgendered George: "*she*," they said indignantly. "Yes, yes. What did *she* wonder?" "*She* wondered if Jeff would tell Rick," they clarified. Notice, here, the response of both Rose and the students to Rose's misgendering of George. It was a brief moment, the students caught it, Rose corrected herself, and the class moved on. Rose and the students model that (1) yes, it happens, people make mistakes without intending to cause harm, (2) calling out that mistake without shaming the mistake maker is a fine thing to do, and (3) correcting oneself immediately and moving on keeps the discussion focused on the story rather than on the person who has made the mistake. The students' reactions also indicated their depth of understanding regarding the importance of gendering people appropriately and the complexity of the identity shift in the story. Their comments served as a sort of impromptu formative assessment in the midst of the larger discussion.

To return to the book, Rose asked the students to consider the adults in the scenes they'd read, including Ms. Udell, George's teacher, who had denied her the role of Charlotte, and how she responded to George as Charlotte on the stage. Doug recalled, "Mrs. Udell . . . gasped. And, I think she was pretty angry because she didn't assign her the part and she didn't know it was going to happen. And she was [headed toward] George [with] a frustrated voice." Rose reread that scene from the book, and Jay interjected, "Ms. Udell, she uh she went into the hall and backstage to go talk to George about it, scowling, and then the principal told her not to? That it was okay." Because Rose remembered the principal had whispered in the teacher's ear, she asked, "Do we know what the principal said to her?" Students shook their heads as Jay insisted, "But it was clearly something to tell her to go away because . . . " Rose filled in, "Because that's what she does." Another student, Molly, added, "It is obviously something convincing. Maybe she said, 'I think George is transgender.'" The idea that the principal would casually share this information struck Jill as unlikely, especially considering the ways that George's identity had been kept a secret for George's own safety. Responding to Molly, she asked, "Do you think that in that moment she said that big thing? [whispering] 'I think George might be transgender.' Or, maybe she said, 'go,' or maybe she said, 'this is going fine.' I mean, do you think she said a big thing [like 'George is transgender]? Or a little thing [like, "let's let George act]?" Peter added, "I think she said something like, 'Let's see how George does.'"

This discussion highlights students' literal and inferential reading comprehension, but it also points to different understandings of transgender identities. Molly's words recognized the power of sharing information about George's identity, but also suggested to Jill that she thought, "If Ms. Udell just knows George is transgender, all will be fine!" Her classmates were more tempered, focusing on ways the principal might have redirected Ms. Udell without sharing that George is transgender. In contrast to Jill's concerns, being transgender might not be a "big thing" in Molly's eyes; one of her teachers is transgender, after all. Being transgender is just another identity, so why wouldn't the principal just let the teacher in on who George is? On the other hand, perhaps Molly doesn't have a realistic sense of how some transgender students experience bigotry at the hands of teachers, leading her to underestimate why a less direct approach might be preferred in this situation. Certainly Jill, Rose, and Molly didn't break all of this down in this discussion, but they made space to question, think about, and critique each other's responses, which led to deeper understanding of the lives of transgender people.

In order to help students better understand these dynamics Rose asked students to act out scenes from this chapter. In the first, the scene described above with Principal Maldanado and Ms. Udell's interaction, there is very little dialogue. Rose read aloud the text and students took turns acting it out. Because they had no lines to read, the student actors focused on their body language.

When Rose read Ms. Udell's reaction to the principal's unknown words, Linus, the 4th-grader playing the role of Ms. Udell cowered in fear in reaction to her boss's words. This prompted Jill to refer them back to a discussion about power and allyship they'd had earlier in the year. She reminded students "how people with power can be allies and they can use that power in different ways." When Linus acted fearful of the principal's words, Jill wondered if those words could have been the principal using her power to change Ms. Udell's actions toward George. Jonas agreed, "Yeah, [the principal] is Ms. Udell's boss, so she'd better not . . . " Nodding, Jill said, "Right! . . . When a boss uses her power to help those with less power in a situation, that can be super important." This led Alice to infer what the principal's experiences had been that might lead her to act as an ally. She said, "Maybe Principal Maldonado has some experiences where she has dealt with this kind of thing before. She knows about this, and she feels empathetic for George because George is in this kind of snit that she can't get out of." Referring to the text, Rose added specific evidence to Alice's claim, saying, "Remember that George noticed the sign in Principal M's office that said something about supportive groups or [safe] spaces for LGBT . . ." Alice nods, "I thought the safe space was important for George." In this scene, the words of the author help highlight the ways that cisgender people can be allies to transgender people, but by using ELA practices to provide students the space to act out what they heard and to discuss that acting, Rose and Jill shed important light on the realities of life for transgender people: School is often not a safe space and allies can make a difference.

Writing Extension Activities. One afternoon, just after finishing *George*, Rose excitedly informed the students that the author, Alex Gino, was doing a reading at a bookstore across the state. It was too far to take the whole class, but she and Jill were planning to attend. After their cries of jealousy died down, Rose told students they could write letters to Gino expressing how they felt about *George* that she and Jill could deliver. They were thrilled. To get them started thinking about their audience for these letters, Rose asked them to share any knowledge they had about Gino. They were surprised to realize that they didn't know much at all about this author of their now favorite text. Students prepared to write their letters by researching who Gino is at the author's website (alexgino.com). During their research, they learned that Gino is transgender and uses the gender neutral pronouns "they/them/their." That meant also learning how to properly address a person in formal writing using these pronouns. This information came from a variety of websites related to language use and gender nonbinary people provided by Rose and Jill, including www.theyismypronoun.com. The class drew on these sites to generate a list of terms and pronoun possibilities that Rose wrote on the board (Hermann-Wilmarth et al., 2017).

After brainstorming ideas for the content of their letters as a prewriting activity, the class gathered together in the meeting area. Rose drew a piece of lined paper on the marker board and began to walk students through the format of a formal letter. When they arrived at the salutation, she asked, "How should we address Alex Gino in a formal way?" The class considered the multiple options they had generated from their research, but eventually settled on Mx. (pronounced "mix") as the most fitting choice because it felt closest to the traditional Mr. or Ms. they would use for a male- or female-identified person. Continuing with direct instruction regarding paragraph structures and finishing with signatures, the students and Rose worked together to fill in the example on the board. She then sent them off to their desks to write their rough drafts. Rose and Jill circulated around the room, redirecting students and answering questions. At one point, Linus tapped Jill on the shoulder. "I have a question: if I write 'I like the gender I was assigned at birth (which is male)' do I put the comma before or after the parenthesis?"

This snippet captures so much of the teaching that occurred in Rose's room, teaching that combines understanding of gender and sexuality with ELA skills. First, Linus demonstrated how he had come to an understanding of the term "gender assigned at birth." During the reading of *George*, Rose and Jill took time to offer definitions to students surrounding gender and sexuality. They wanted to ensure students understood that Melissa didn't just *believe* she was a girl, but that she *was* a girl. Students knew, therefore, that the "gender a person is assigned at birth" is when someone is born and a doctor or nurse tells the room "it's a boy!" or "it's a girl!" "For example," Jill had explained, "I was assigned female at birth, and that assignment matches who I know myself to be. For George, this is not the case. A doctor assigned her 'boy' when she was born, but she knows that not to be true." Defining terms in this way was a part of the novel study, and in Linus's letter, his conception of the important layers of gender and identity became obvious.

Rose and Jill also wanted students to understand that the identities that they claim are valued. Resistance to including books with LGBTQ characters sometimes comes with the worry that students will be persuaded to become LGBTQ or that they will feel devalued if they are straight and/or cisgender. Linus's words, "I like the gender I was assigned at birth" reflect the class's conversations around gender and gender identity that affirmed people's own sense of who they are. It was important to Rose that no particular way of living gender was put down or idealized in the classroom, whether that expression was cisgender or more gender creative, but that students felt comfortable with their own personal identities. As Rose told the students many times, "You can like traditional girl things if you are a girl! But what's important to remember is that you don't have to." We can see this valuing of one's own identity in Linus's words.

Finally, we also see evidence of Rose's grammar teaching in this short sentence. Daily practice through individual and classwide correction of sentences written on the board were a part of morning work. In planning his writing, Linus attended to sentence structure, the use of commas and parentheses, and the use of complete sentences. Linus reminds us that even this direct grammar teaching can easily go hand in hand with content that is inclusive of LGBTQ identities.

Looking Across the Novel Study

Even a year later, when Jill asked the 5th-graders if the book they were currently reading was their favorite that they'd read during their 2 years with Rose, one student smiled and, thinking back fondly to her 4th-grade year said she liked it fine, but "it's no *George!*" A story as compelling to students as *George* can serve to ease teacher worries about including transgender people in elementary ELA. Students in this class universally loved the book.

So what helped Rose and her students build their love of the book? Before they began reading, Rose and Jill scaffolded their students' learning by exploring gender and how it works in language and daily life. As they began reading, they also made a point to define and discuss key terms related to transgender people (Hermann-Wilmarth et al., 2017). This scaffolding created initial understandings that allowed for more substantive discussion of the text. Students' independent written reflections for homework helped them try out and apply these new terms in their own thinking.

During this study, Rose had Jill's support in defining words and leading activities. For teachers who are themselves less familiar with LGBTQ-related topics, community LGBTQ centers or other local organizations can be good sources of support. Sites that might offer such support are listed in the Conclusion. Furthermore, information collected during the postreading research into gender-neutral pronouns was new for both teachers. Showing students that teachers are willing to learn alongside them can be a powerful experience for all members of the classroom.

Throughout this novel study, just as in novel studies you might have taught, students had space to talk about the characters and topics, write in independent yet structured ways, and were required to return to the text to support their claims and ideas. Expanding representations to include transgender people in this kind of format is thus simultaneously totally new, and yet completely routine.

STOP AND THINK

When you consider doing this kind of work in your own classroom, it can be helpful to think about how you are already engaged in practices you can build on. That work can help you expand representations by including (more) LGBTQ texts through novel studies.

- How do you already address issues of social justice in your classroom? What other types of difference can you use to help students connect LGBTQ topics to other situations where people are treated or seen in an unfair light?
- What about the conversations and ideas that Rose's students had feel familiar to you and your students? What about that familiarity helps you see this as work that you want to do in your teaching?
- What questions do you still have?

Part II

QUESTIONING CATEGORIES BY READING STRAIGHT BOOKS THROUGH A QUEER LENS

> *Jesse:* You can't exchange a girl to be a boy.
> *Michael:* I can't do this in my mind. A girl does girl stuff.
> *Darius:* Like, boys cannot have long hair. Long hair means girl.
> *Anthony:* Yeah, like braids. Braids are girl.
> *Ms. O'Grady:* But some boys in this class have braids! Look around!
> *Anthony:* Nope, boys CANNOT have braids. Well, actually, I do have a cousin who has braids. But, boys can't wear beads.
> *Ms. O'Grady:* But, I know some boys who wear beads, too.
> *Anthony:* Well, okay, then boys can't wear barrettes.
>
> —2nd-grade students and their teacher, Ms. O'Grady

Barbara O'Grady, the teacher in this racially diverse, midwestern public school 2nd-grade class, made it a practice to lead her students in a daily read-aloud after lunch. On the day of the above conversation, they were well into *Because of Winn Dixie* (DiCamillo, 2009). Barbara had stopped to ask her students how the book would be similar or different if India Opal, the protagonist, was a boy rather than a girl. As they talked, students used their critical thinking skills to ponder the suggestion, connect what they knew to what their teacher had asked, and evaluate her proposal. Likewise, they drew on evidence from their lives, critiqued the arguments of others, and made a series of claims and rebuttals based on opposing evidence. In addition to these ELA skills, however, they were also questioning the categories of "boy" and "girl," who fit in them, how they were identified, and why those boundaries mattered.

In Part I, we explored how teachers can include representations of LGBTQ people in their classroom materials. We also shared how that approach has some limitations and drawbacks, particularly for people in contexts where their discussion of LGBTQ topics is clearly challenging or risky. In Part II, we introduce you to another approach to more inclusive ELA teaching: questioning categories. By this, we mean directing students' attention to the ways in which categories and labels, particularly around gender and sexuality, are created, maintained, and seen as normal even when they are much more complicated in our real lives. This is the kind of teaching and learning Barbara and her students were doing.

Using this approach, teachers can teach students to notice how taken-for-granted assumptions shape the media we consume, language we use, books we read, and ways we expect people to participate in the world. Specifically, this means learning about diverse gender identities and sexual orientations even when reading books that don't include explicitly named LGBTQ characters (Ryan & Hermann-Wilmarth, 2013). For this reason, we see this approach as a gateway into LGBTQ-inclusive teaching for teachers who are new to this work. These methods open a starting point for people who are not yet comfortable with, ready for, or able to teach using direct representations of LGBTQ people in their classrooms, whether those restrictions stem from mandated curricula or district policies and community norms that preclude openly LGBTQ-themed books. Even though they do not directly acknowledge LGBTQ identities, these starting points are still valuable. When moments related to gender and sexual orientation in texts are highlighted by teachers, students have opportunities to consider how these categories apply to *all* people, not just LGBTQ people. We believe this approach can offer flexibility to teachers who are interested in inclusive teaching but find themselves in explicitly challenging contexts in terms of openness to LGBTQ topics, all while using more traditional books already found on many classroom and library shelves.

CHAPTER 4

Discussing Queer Moments in Straight Books

If we ask you to think of an elementary school teacher, what's the image that comes to mind? If your thoughts are anything like the results of a Google image search of the term, you would picture young White women in cardigans with children gathered at their feet. This intersection of race, gender, class, age, and ability is pervasive in the image of who teachers of young children are. But now, think about all the teachers you've ever met or seen or heard of or could imagine. How many other "versions" of teacher are or could there be in reality?

Even if we move away from people, what is the image that you conjure when we say "elementary school classroom?" Is it like Jill's first classroom: a rickety portable trailer with too many desks and a bulletin board crawling with ants stubbornly eating the student work stapled in neat lines across it? Or do you think of a classroom like the one she visits regularly now: a spacious, windowed room, full of bright colors with a carpet in one corner for class meetings and bean bag chairs for kids to sit in while they read books from one of the many shelves? Of course, not all classrooms fit either of these two examples. Does the classroom in your mind's eye fit somewhere within the range created by the two described classrooms or is it so different that it's outside of these examples altogether?

By thinking in this way, you've just taken an initial step in learning to *queer*—mess up and complicate—the categories of "elementary school teacher" and "elementary school classroom" (Britzman, 1995; J. Butler, 1999; Foucault, 1977/1995). You first considered what most easily came to mind with regard to these labels that you are familiar with and live with every day. Then you thought about all the real-life situations that don't fit that idealized example. This helped you notice complications to the category that are always there, even if they're not the first things that come to mind.

That's the kind of "messy" thinking that students can also be taught to do. When teachers and students learn to notice and "mess up" categories— particularly those related to bodies, gender, sexual orientation, and love— as they read, write, and talk in their ELA classrooms, they are making those categories more inclusive. By approaching literacy and language arts in this way, teachers can help students question the systems that exclude LGBTQ people without ever even using the words *gay, lesbian, bisexual,* or *transgender.* The key to teaching about LGBTQ topics without explicitly reading or writing or talking about LGBTQ people is in putting our attention on the *categories* that shape our identities in the first place (Staley & Leonardi, 2016; Sumara & Davis, 1998; Wargo, 2017). Once we notice those categories, how they work, and the power they have over how we see ourselves and the world, we can practice thinking in ways that make those categories more inclusive of more people. In the rest of this chapter, we will explain more about this approach, why it's useful for teachers and students, and, perhaps most importantly, what it can look like in actual elementary school classrooms.

THE IMPORTANCE OF CATEGORIES

Categories and labels matter. They give us information about the world and provide a system for classifying that information. They help us know how to act in particular situations. Categorizing people can provide a sense of identity and connection. As helpful as categories might be, however, they also tend to mask the diversity that exists within them. They draw lines around who is "in" and who is "out." When we fall outside the lines they create, we may hide the parts of us that feel weird or different from others in order to be seen as part of the group. Or we may feel like we have to defend who we are or what we do. Do you ever have a nagging sense that you aren't quite "like" other teachers you know, whether it's because of how you look, what you wear, where or what you teach, how you do parts of your job, or even how you feel about your job? Being outside or on the edges of a category can be emotionally challenging.

Categories are also arranged relative to one another. A pair of categories that are matched together, like the opposites that we teach to little kids, is called a *binary*. Examples of binary categories include "woman" and "man" for gender, "person of color" and "White" for race, "rich" and "poor" for socioeconomic status, "disabled" and "able-bodied" for physical ability, or "gay" and "straight" for sexual orientation. In binary categories, each of the two terms are seen as half of the binary that, locked together, make a whole. In this thinking, part of the definition of a woman is "not a man," and part of the definition of man is "not a woman." The problem is, the two "halves" aren't usually equal. In most binaries, one category has more social power than the other (Britzman, 1995; J. Butler, 1999; Kumashiro, 2002). So, historically, White people in the United States have had more social power than people of color.

Rich people have had more social power than poor people. Men have had more social power than women. And straight people have had more social power than gay people. So these terms organize our world. They persist because they give us a sense of "this-over-that" and "this-but-not-that" that we use to make decisions about who belongs with whom and who should act in what ways.

But these terms aren't always as helpful as we sometimes think they are. The binary terms for race listed above, for example, don't account well for people who are biracial. The binary terms for gender don't account well for people who are transgender. In fact, just like you found when you thought about the category of "elementary school teacher," *all* of these categories are much messier than they seem at first.

Let's take gender as an example. As we did with "elementary school teacher," we can think about our initial impressions of a category like "woman" or "man." But we also know those categories are really diverse. What, exactly, does a "woman" look like? Or what activities or clothes are "for" men? All the answers we can come up with quickly fall apart when we think about the range of people in the world. Are men with long hair not men? Are women who serve in traditionally male occupations not women? Even if we think more specifically about bodies, are women who have had hysterectomies or mastectomies no longer women? What about transgender people who were assigned one gender at birth but who identify as and live as another gender? Even if you have personal beliefs about how the people described here should be classified, it's still true that there's a good deal of variation and more gray area then we might initially anticipate. Our lived realities are almost always more complicated than these binary categories suggest, so when we forget to notice the diversity within and among those terms, we miss out on understanding that variation and so miss out on seeing or understanding actual people.

The Connected Categories of the Heterosexual Matrix

Not only do identity categories come in binaries, but some of those binaries get connected to others. Categories of gender, for example, are interrelated with categories about bodies and sexuality (J. Butler, 1999). In other words, our lives are shaped not just by the binary categories themselves, but by these "stacks" of categories that assume particular things about who we are or should be. Gender theorists call this set of stacked categories the *heterosexual matrix* (J. Butler, 1999; Rich, 1980). This idea says that biological sex, gender, and sexuality are all interrelated sets of binaries. In our society, we assume that bodies born male (sex) identify as men and act masculine (gender) and fall in love with women (sexuality). The other side of the binary says that we assume that bodies born female (sex) identify as women and act feminine (gender) and fall in love with men (sexuality). Because they are so interconnected, challenging the boundaries of one of the categories can make the whole structure shaky. Like squeezing a balloon and seeing the air puff out at the other end, the expansion or narrowing of one category necessarily creates an effect on all of the others because of their interconnections. The process of noticing and then expanding the categories of the heterosexual matrix in ways that disrupt their binary opposition is what we mean by *queering* (Britzman, 1995; Kidd, 1998; Ryan & Hermann-Wilmarth, 2013; Sumara & Davis, 1998).

How Kids' Lives are Shaped by the Heterosexual Matrix

The matrix—and its shakiness—can be useful when thinking about children because it gives us a mechanism for recognizing how gender and sexuality are related. While we might not be comfortable thinking about children's sexuality, we certainly recognize gender as a category that clearly and explicitly applies to children in our society. From before birth, we have a sense that people can be organized around binary categories of gender. It is, after all, usually one of the first questions we ask pregnant women or new parents: "Is it a boy or a girl?" But this sense of gender has a connection to other matrix categories. It's the reason, for example, that some parents won't let their sons play dress-up or have their nails painted: it might "make" him gay. If a girl doesn't act "ladylike," she might be called a tomboy, but she could just as easily be teased for being a lesbian. In this way, markers of gender extrapolate in people's minds to sexual orientation. That's the matrix at work.

Like pulling out a key Jenga block and watching the whole tower fall, the matrix suggests that changes to any part of it affect the whole thing. Specifically, it means that when we work with students to expand their ideas around gender—about what things are "boy" or "girl" things, about what boys and girls should look like or act like or do and what they shouldn't look like or act like or do—we are working through a familiar category they live everyday toward an expansion that would also allow a boy to fall in love with a boy or a girl to fall in love with a girl. In other words, if we acknowledge that the categories of "boy" and "girl" are complicated and expansive, then there is room in those categories for "boys" and "girls" to dress, self-identify as, and love whomever and however they want. In this way, we're working through the parts of the matrix that are most applicable to children's lives in order to help them come to new understandings about the whole system. When we move away from ideas of gender and sexuality that are predetermined by the matrix, we are doing queer work that makes space for more people.

STOP AND THINK

- Where does your school rely on gender to structure the details of students' days at school? How might that structure be hard for kids who don't fit easily in these categories?
- Where and how do students receive messages about who they are supposed to fall in love with or how families are supposed to be? Do the talk and rituals in your classroom expand or restrict those possibilities for students' lives?
- What assumptions are made about boys and girls in the texts and other materials used most frequently in your school and classroom?

DOING THE WORK OF QUESTIONING CATEGORIES

Like with expanding representations in Part I, there are a variety of options for starting out with questioning categories in ELA instruction. If a teacher is using children's literature, the process of queering taken-for-granted categories can mean directing readers' attention to places where gender, sexuality, bodies, and love do not all line up neatly into stereotypical expectations for all characters. Teachers can also help students question cultural norms about who gets to fall in love, who gets to be in families, who gets teased for not being the right "type" of boy or girl, and how people are grouped together or left out of a group based on their bodies, gender, or sexuality. The goal is to use familiar teaching materials to notice and expand categories in the heterosexual matrix, thereby exposing the systems that exclude LGBTQ people. With this kind of teaching, elementary classrooms can become spaces that address experiences many LGBTQ people have, even in the absence of books with LGBTQ characters or direct discussions of LGBTQ identities.

Finding Entry Points to Help You Get Started

For the remainder of this chapter, we look to ways teachers have found small moments in which to notice and expand the categories of the heterosexual matrix in their ELA teaching. These are moments that happened quickly—even spontaneously—or as one shorter lesson within a larger book study. We hope that by reading about how teachers found and took advantage of these fleeting moments within their curriculum, readers will begin to imagine similar small places in their own teaching where categories of gender and sexuality can be expanded. It is our experience that these small opportunities to question categories often have a ripple effect that reaches well beyond the lesson itself in ways teachers could not plan for or imagine.

First, we show you Rose's 4th/5th-grade class that looked more closely at the ways gender categories are reinforced by the language we use. Then, we see Barbara's 2nd-grade classroom that explored students' developing understanding of gender expression while reading *Because of Winn-Dixie*. And finally, we visit Maree's 5th-grade class whose reading of the historical fiction novel *Crooked River* surprisingly helped them think about the ways gender works—and could be expanded—in their everyday lives. In all three cases, finding and exploring these "queer moments" in the course of everyday, familiar ELA teaching practices began to shift students' awareness and understanding of the taken-for-granted categories that shape their lives, including those related to gender and sexuality.

Queering Oral Language: Seeing It in Practice. Toward the end of the school year in Rose's 4th/5th-grade class, she and Jill, who was coteaching three afternoons a week, wanted students to explore how gender shapes our language. They wanted students to understand what it might be like to internally monitor what information people make public about themselves by simply speaking.

They initiated this conversation by defining pronouns and then asking students about the pronouns they use for themselves. Jill asked the students to partner up and tell each other about their day, but without using words that would indicate a person's gender. She and Rose suggested that students clap if their partner slipped up. As they talked together, the air was filled with claps and the voices of children correcting themselves, giggling as they realized how hard this activity was. After a few minutes, they circled back up as a whole group.

The first student to participate began by telling the class that this was super easy. "I just went to piano lessons with my mom." When the whole class clapped once, the student looked around confused. When Jill asked why they clapped, students responded in uncoordinated unison: "Mom! Mom! He said 'mom'!"

This moved the class into a discussion about how the word *mom* assumes a particular gender, and while the student's argument that he didn't say "she," "her," or "hers" was true and valid, the rest of the class recognized that in our common comprehension of the word, *mom* indicates "female parent." This discussion invited the class to explore how even words that are not pronouns can reference a person's gender. As she was leading the discussion, Jill herself inadvertently used gendered pronouns. As the students clapped her into silence, they saw how all of us are shaped by this language, even when we are consciously trying to notice it. To wrap up, Jill asked the students to think about this question: Now that they saw how frequently gendered language was used, how would it feel if you were constantly referred to with language that didn't match the gender you know yourself to be? This question helped move from their own experiences to the experiences of those with LGBTQ identities, even without reading about or naming LGBTQ identities.

This short teaching moment was just a blip in the life of this classroom, but the work it did was powerful. For the rest of that year and into the next, students referred to this activity and paid particular attention to their use of gendered language in their talk and writing. The point, for Jill and Rose, wasn't to eliminate students' use of gendered language, but to help students see how pervasive gender is in our talk, and to consider what it might be like to be misgendered over and over again on a daily basis and the kind of effort it takes to try to change or expand those common meanings. Even if your classroom is not a place where future intentional conversations about transgender people will occur, helping your students notice how gender is at play in their own lives might give them a way to think about it differently.

Building a Habit of Discussing Queer Moments: Seeing It in Practice. As in many schools, Barbara's 2nd-grade classroom is shaped by frequent interruptions and copious external accountability measures. Barbara remains responsible for helping her students meet benchmarks and standards, even if the context in which she teaches and the contexts in which her students have been asked to learn have made that level of achievement elusive thus far. It may appear that this is an impossible—or at least improbable—context in which to spend time questioning the categories of gender and sexuality. Barbara can't add a new unit to her curriculum. She can't even read a book outside of what her administration expects. Many people in her school community would not support her use of LGBTQ-inclusive materials. But Barbara says, "My kids see gay people in their neighborhoods. . . . And we have to somehow have conversations about this difference that isn't talked about. And, my kids need to know that no matter who you are, you're still a person, and we need to treat people with respect and dignity."

Therefore, it is in classrooms like Barbara's that questioning categories can be especially useful: She can connect it to straight books that were already a part of her classroom practice, even for just a quick 10 minutes of read-aloud time, in order to question the category of gender. This way, Barbara can read the same texts as the others in her grade level, but still look for places related to gender categories in the text and explore those with her students when they come up.

One particularly productive use of this strategy came during a reading of *Because of Winn Dixie* (DiCamillo, 2009) when Barbara asked her students to imagine that the main character, a girl named India Opal, was a boy. Because India Opal's actions in the text aren't particularly gendered, Barbara wondered how much of a stretch this exercise would be. She was surprised when her students outright refused to imagine it, as shared in the scene introducing Part II.

Their line for this gendered division kept moving as their discussion and real-life examples ("But my cousin does!") stretched their previous understanding of the categories. Barbara's students were able to revise their boundaries—based on hairstyle—for who could be a girl and who could be a boy. Recalling Souto-Manning and her students from Chapter 2 (Souto-Manning & Hermann-Wilmarth, 2008), Barbara's goal was not to create students who all had the same understanding of gender, but this 5-minute discussion, stolen during a day full of mandated curriculum, created space for students to think differently about gender. That her students were "moving the line" means that they were, indeed, questioning—and expanding—gendered categories.

Barbara also snuck moments of questioning categories into the more externally mandated areas of her teaching. For example, when introducing a new leveled text to a reading group, a student indicated that the alligator on the cover was a girl. Barbara took time to ask the student, "How do you know?" When students suggested that the presence of a purple hair bow indicated femaleness, Barbara again made the pedagogical decision to help students question this category, asking the group, "Are some colors girl colors and some colors boy colors?"

Students took her inquiry seriously. Some were sure that purple was a girl color, and some thought that boys and girls could both like purple. When one male student was adamant that boys could not wear purple, another was upset because his favorite colors were pink and purple. The group eventually came to an agreement that purple was really neutral because one of their favorite male pop stars liked purple, but they all insisted that boys could not wear bows, no matter the color. Another student, again moving the line, proposed that toys were different from colors, so there were definitely boy toys and girl toys. This time, his classmates, not Barbara, challenged and disagreed with him. He asked about dolls and whether they were just for girls. Another student agreed, alluding to her own family's rules about who was and was not allowed to play with dolls. The students didn't reach any kind of consensus at this point, and Barbara realized she had to move on with the reading lesson at hand, so she redirected their attention. This infiltration of gender talk into basal reading groups was one bridge between what's possible in more unrestricted read-aloud times and the rest of the heavily monitored and assessed parts of the school day. Barbara pushed herself to locate and take advantage of these moments frequently during her literacy block.

Nevertheless, Barbara was often left wondering if she'd done enough. She felt like many of the conversations just dissolved. When they occurred in 5-minute bursts and were bookended by the kinds of accountability expectations that put pressure on time and materials, this kind of pedagogical work sometimes felt incomplete or unfinished. But Barbara's classroom shows that when teachers repeatedly find and take advantage of such smaller moments, they can string together and influence students' thinking. Her class's developing conversations show how even small discussions can create context for future talk and shape their perspectives.

For example, rather than reading *Because of Winn Dixie* one particular afternoon, Barbara used their read-aloud time to ask students to draw images of how they imagined three of the characters: India Opal and the Dewberry brothers, two boys who tease India Opal in the story. As they busily worked, Barbara and Jill wandered among the students. Both teachers noticed that most students had drawn India Opal wearing either a skirt or a dress. After pointing this out to her students, Barbara asked all of the females in the room who were wearing dresses or skirts to stand up. As both teachers were wearing pants, they both quickly headed for chairs, and watched the students wait for anyone to stand. Nobody did.

When Barbara asked, "If none of you are wearing a skirt or a dress, why do you think India Opal was?" the students had no answer. So Barbara turned back to the text and asked them to consider the kinds of activities that India Opal does in the story. The list they came up with ranged from walking her dog to going to the library. Barbara then asked students to connect their own lives to India Opal's by asking, "Do you wear a skirt when you do the things India Opal does?" The students shook their heads, but hypothesized that maybe it was hot in *Because of Winn Dixie* and, since dresses are more comfortable in the summer than pants, she would wear a skirt. "Wait," Jill interjected, "could boys wear dresses in the summer? It *is* so much more comfortable!" This suggestion was met with verbal disgust. One student summed it up succinctly, "Dresses are for *girls*." Jill explained how pants used to be only for boys and girls and women couldn't wear them, and the girls in the room exchanged looks of shock.

This led back to the kinds of conversations they'd had in several small moments over previous weeks. Again, the teachers asked, "So are there other things that are just for girls?" and again, much like in the reading group, several male students suggested dolls were definitely a girls-only item and they'd get in trouble if they played with them. Jill asked, "How do you treat boys who do?" Barbara added, "How do we treat people who do things that we aren't used to?" The response was a long silence. Barbara wrapped up the conversation by saying, "That's your challenge. We're going to talk about this for the next few days. I want you to notice people who do things that you're not used to. We're going to talk about how we treat all kinds of people." And, with that, she transitioned the students and their conversations to their reading centers.

This was another short conversation, but because it built on previous talk, it went a little further. This time, Barbara was able to prompt students to action. She extended conversations about language, colors, toys, and characters into students' own lives and treatment of people who, through the ways that they live, question categories. By continually revisiting discussions centered on gender, even in brief instances, Barbara let her students know that these ideas were important and deserved their attention. They might only get to it in tiny moments, but over the course of a school year, these bits, strung together, had power. There was a progression in how long the students engaged with these ideas, their willingness to question taken-for-granted understandings of what was and was not acceptable with regard to gender, and the ways Barbara found to resolve the discussions.

Finding spaces to integrate discussions of gender or sexuality doesn't need to be thought of in terms of being a whole unit or something that takes over one's entire curriculum. Small moments collected over time, like those in Barbara's class, create long-lasting understanding. Barbara's school community, perhaps like yours, wasn't necessarily open to reading books with explicitly LGBTQ characters. But because Barbara was invested in expanding her students' perspectives, she revisited important questions around the construction of categories related to gender with her students. She asked them to reconsider what they had always assumed and to use people and places around them and in the books they read as evidence to stretch their thinking. Though there were times when these conversations felt unresolved, they opened up thinking around the policing of and rules about this social category of the heterosexual matrix. This helped destabilize the seemingly fixed categories of the matrix and reaffirm that taken-for-granted representations can, and should, be questioned.

Capitalizing on Unexpected Queer Moments: Seeing It in Practice. Although Maree taught ELA to her 5th-grade students in ways that occasionally included representations of LGBTQ people, she had no plans to address LGBTQ topics during an integrated ELA/Social Studies unit that covered the colonization of the Ohio River Valley in the early 1800s. In this unit, Maree had planned ways for students to explore textbooks, informational texts, and leveled texts about this time period. She had also devised a variety of writing assignments that would allow students to synthesize and communicate what they learned. Anchoring the unit would be her full-class read-aloud, *Crooked River* (Pearsall, 2005), a historical fiction novel set in the Ohio frontier in 1812. One day toward the end of the unit, while Caitlin was coteaching with her, Maree unexpectedly stumbled on a queer moment as she read one of the final chapters of *Crooked River* aloud to the class. Stopping and discussing this moment in the text gave her students an opportunity to question and challenge the categories of the heterosexual matrix.

The book's primary narrator is Rebecca, a young White girl, who saw the White settlers of her town accuse a Native American (Ojibwe) man named Amik of a crime he did not commit. As Rebecca gets to know more about Amik, his family, and the ways he's been treated by the White settlers, she gets increasingly outraged at the injustice of the situation. Eventually, she decides to sneak into town to sabotage the gallows set up for Amik's execution. As part of this plot, Rebecca realizes it will be safer for her to dress like a boy in her brother's clothes when she goes into town to prevent any undue attention she would receive as a girl traveling alone. Maree read from the book, "As I [Rebecca] pulled on Lorenzo's worn trousers and his old linen shirt, I tried not to think about how I was destined to go straight to hell if any man caught sight of the shameful clothes I was wearing" and heard giggles. She paused, and together, the class talked about why it would be so bad for Rebecca to be dressed in boys' clothes. The students spoke fairly generally about how historical expectations for clothing were different for boys than girls: Girls had to wear skirts and boys had to wear pants so it would be breaking a cultural norm to do it any differently.

Picking up on students' reactions to the situation in the text and on the conversation they'd just had, Maree said to the class: "But wait. Back then, it was bad for Rebecca to be in boys' clothes, like pants. So bad she was worried about being sent to hell! But look around our classroom. I'm wearing pants. Lots of the girls are wearing pants. So that's a rule that's changed since this story took place." The students all nodded in agreement; they felt that that rule had definitely changed. Maree continued, "Here's my question for you: Have the old rules for *boys* changed in the same way? Why can girls wear pants now, but boys still can't wear skirts and dresses without being laughed at? Why has only one rule changed over time but not the other?" At first, students sat, stunned, with questioning and puzzled looks on their faces. They couldn't say for sure why rules for girls would have changed so much while rules for boys had stayed the same. One student said, "I don't really know how to put this, it's just that . . ." before trailing off without finishing her thought. Another student pointed out that boys *could* wear skirts, especially if they "wanted to stand out" or if they wore a kilt, but that it just wasn't very common. Maree agreed, saying, "That's true. It's more traditional for men to wear skirts—like kilts—in some places," but she then challenged them to keep thinking about this idea of "standing out" and why, for most guys, wearing a skirt wasn't something that was accepted as normal.

Finally, more directly, she asked students, "When you see or hear of a guy wearing a skirt, what do people assume [about him]?" Students quietly but immediately answered, "That he's gay." Here, the students' responses demonstrated their familiarity with the idea that, for many people, the way that a person expresses their gender through clothing is assumed to be indicative of their sexual orientation. In other words, students' discussion of Maree's questions helped them notice and question connections between the interrelated matrix categories of gender and sexuality.

Even after they left the read-aloud carpet, students continued to process the ways gender is often falsely assumed as an indicator of sexuality. Many of them were uncomfortable allowing such assumptions to stand. They wanted to find a way to expand and pull apart the matrix categories to make more space for more people to be comfortable experimenting with gender separate from any resulting assumptions about other parts of their identities. Later that afternoon, a group of the class's most popular boys came up with an idea. Given the ways that rules around clothing had changed for girls but not for boys, they asked Caitlin if they could "propose a dress and skirt day for our school." The boys sat down together in front of a computer with Caitlin behind them for any additional guidance they'd need, and (after much deliberation about who would get to say "please excuse the interruption"!), this is the PA announcement they composed:

> *Ace:* Please excuse the interruption. My name is Ace.
> *Harry:* My name is Harry.
> *Kevin:* My name is Kevin.
> *Paul:* And I'm Paul.
> *Harry:* We're here to tell you about our made-up holiday that is on March 5.
> *Kevin:* This is optional for everybody in the school.
> *Paul:* On this day boys and girls can feel good about wearing the other gender's clothes. Gender means the ways a boy or a girl lives.
> *Ace:* Just so you "boys" don't feel left out you can shop in the girls' section and wear girl clothes.
> *Harry:* And girls can wear boy's clothes too.
> *Kevin:* This does not mean you have to change your physical appearance, but you can change your clothes.
> *Paul:* We got this inspiration from a book called *Crooked River* by Shelley Pearsall.
> *All:* We hope you participate!

Throughout their composition process, they kept checking in with each other to be sure they were accomplishing their goal of expanding people's experiences with gender. At Caitlin's prompting, they talked at length about their audience and how the announcement would have to do some of the teaching they'd already experienced in Maree's class, especially around what gender means. They also were deliberate about attending to both sides of the gender binary; it was important to them that both girls and boys knew they could disrupt traditional clothing choices.

In their exchange, the boys talked a lot about freedom: freedom to dress how you wanted on this day, but, relatedly, freedom from the gender policing and assumptions about sexuality that traditionally accompany such transgressive behaviors in schools like those the students had named in their discussion with Maree. Through their reading and writing, these popular, cisgender boys encountered a "queer" moment in a "straight" text where the system of biology and gender and sexuality didn't line up as usual. That situation in the book, along with Maree's mediation and questions, created a chance for these boys to question, explore, play with, and even advocate for the subversion of gender categories as they were traditionally lived in their school.

Finding Familiar ELA Practices in This New Teaching

The portraits of teaching provided in these three classrooms give concrete examples of what questioning categories might look like in a range of contexts. As in our classroom examples of expanding representations, these teachers and students found different ways to try out the questioning categories approach. They were taught to different students in different places with different texts and by teachers facing different kinds of restrictions and accountability mandates. They were sometimes brief moments, but they all came from a teacher's willingness to use the space and tools of the ELA curriculum to engage students in deep thinking around important ideas that shape their own lives.

Even if the idea of queering is new to you, some of what you saw in these examples was likely familiar—you might read aloud to your own students during stolen moments in the day or use historical fiction to bring your social studies curriculum to life. If you teach in a school where each learning activity you undertake must be tied directly to a recognizable (or research-based) literacy practice, these classroom examples included several common methods you could also employ. For example, Rose and Jill led their students in oral language study. Barbara and Maree accomplished much of their conversation with students during interactive read-alouds of children's literature. Barbara even found space for discussion during the text preview of a guided reading lesson while she was activating students' background knowledge. In all three of these classrooms, children shared their thinking in group and peer-to-peer discussions. The questions the teachers asked were higher-level, open-ended questions that encouraged critical thinking and the use of evidence to support their ideas. Barbara even tried a sketch-to-stretch activity (Whitin, 2002) where students visually represented their thinking as a scaffold for their talk. The discussions teachers led encouraged students to explore multiple perspectives, notice character traits, make text-to-self connections and disconnections (Jones, Clarke, & Enriquez, 2010), and compare changes across various time periods of history. What is important about the pedagogical choices made in these classrooms is that the content of these familiar literacy practices also drew attention to the construction of what is "normal" around the various identity categories of the heterosexual matrix.

The books these teachers read and the activities they led are not the only ways to explore queer moments in texts. The questions below, developed from Hermann-Wilmarth and Ryan (2015a), are a tool to help you build your own queer lens when reading straight texts. They point out elements to look for and questions to ask that can guide you and your students to these kinds of queer moments in your own teaching.

> *For plot:* Does the plot rely on adherence to gender norms? How is the story shaped by the characters' refusal to conform to social norms? What happens when characters break social rules?
>
> *For setting:* Do characters move between different worlds with different rules? What determines the differences? Do they explore and try to name those rules that dictate behaviors in different places?
>
> *For characters:* Are characters marginalized for not conforming to gender norms? Do characters struggle to define themselves or resist others' definitions? Does the way the characters look to others match the way the characters understand themselves? What happens if the characters ask others to see them the way they want to be seen? What happens if characters want something forbidden?

STOP AND THINK

How might the examples shared in this chapter be instructive as you consider ways of queering oral language and build a habit of finding queer moments in classroom texts?

- Try for yourself the activity Rose, Jill, and their students did describing your weekend or your family with only gender-neutral language to explore intersections between language and gender. How does this help you think about how gender shapes our language and understandings about people's identities?
- Have you read *The Evolution of Calpurnia Tate* (Kelly, 2009) with your upper elementary class? Or has your early elementary class studied Kevin Henkes? Consider how Calpurnia in Kelly's book, or Chester and Wilson in Henke's *Chester's Way* (1988) break social rules with regard to gender. How could you and your students think about the ways these characters challenge what it means to be a girl or a boy? What happens to the characters? What would happen if the students in your class or school bent gender rules in the same ways?

CONSIDERATIONS AND CHALLENGES IN YOUR CONTEXT

The challenge, for many readers, likely will be learning how to notice the kinds of moments that are worth exploring and queering. There's no firm guide for this, but some big ideas, including the questions listed in the preceding section, can help teachers develop a way of looking at their teaching that help make these kinds of moments more visible. These kinds of questions might not apply to all texts, but they can provide some guidelines for refocusing the ways teachers talk about the queer potential of books already in their ELA curriculum. The more teachers look for these moments and pay attention to the ways students respond, the more opportunities will become visible.

Like all teaching methods, questioning categories has both advantages and disadvantages. While this approach offers a more flexible, nuanced approach to LGBTQ topics than the expanding representations method, the fact that it doesn't explicitly name LGBTQ identities can, in practice, present some drawbacks. First, sometimes the subtlety of this kind of work can be too abstract and implicit for students. For example, they might not always see the connection between an expansion of gender categories and the experiences of LGBTQ people. The small shifts of these experiences might not be enough to change their understanding of the matrix as a whole. Also, while the flexibility offered in this approach can be useful for certain contexts, not naming LGBTQ identities could inadvertently contribute to the silences that already exist in elementary schools around these identities, possibly even reinforcing the idea that it's wrong to talk about LGBTQ people.

The questioning categories approach, however, can be helpful in contexts where school communities are unwelcoming to reading about or discussing explicitly named LGBTQ identities (see the Conclusion for community resources if this is the case in your school). With this approach, students and teachers have the opportunity to challenge cultural norms that keep the heterosexual matrix in place without having to rely on books that might be censored in their community. Likewise, teachers who identify as LGBTQ, even in contexts where their identities are allowed, might feel safer using this approach because they might feel less implicated in talking about broader categories. Finally, questioning categories also invites *all* students and teachers, regardless of their identities, to rethink what they already know about how the categories of the heterosexual matrix are at work in their lives. This opens possibilities for connection between those with different identities through engagement around taken-for-granted notions of gender and sexuality, even with students who might discriminate against LGBTQ people.

You now know about two different approaches to making your ELA classroom more inclusive of LGBTQ identities. We know that not all approaches will work for all teachers at all times, but we hope that you're thinking about ways to locate yourself amid these various possibilities. The final approach in this book, questioning representations, brings together the two methods we've already discussed. It involves doing the queering work of questioning categories while using books *with* LGBTQ characters. We'll explore what that could look like in Part III. Before that, however, we look more closely into Rose and Maree's classrooms to look at how they each used the questioning categories approach to frame larger units of study, creating learning spaces where, often without teacher prompting, students were actively engaged in challenging and expanding notions of gender and sexuality.

CHAPTER 5

Building Students' Queer Lenses Through Anchor Lessons

In this chapter, we highlight ways that teachers can, over time, help students develop a queer lens of their own so that questioning categories becomes a way that students read the world (Freire & Macedo, 1987). To do this we showcase teachers intentionally planning anchor lessons on this topic that their classes could return to as a touchstone throughout the year. Specifically, we look at anchor lessons that Maree taught to her 3rd-grade students and Jill taught to Rose's 4th/5th-grade students around Jacqueline Woodson's (2001) *The Other Side*. We show two classrooms using the same book so that readers can see a multiplicity of responses that students might have. Not only do we look across three grades, but we look in depth at what can happen when students notice how gender is constructed and informs the choices they have. We will see how the concepts built during those anchor lessons threaded through students' subsequent learning, bringing the work of questioning categories to other topics and texts. For these teachers, the use of a queer lens while reading this straight text, along with accompanying pre- and postreading ELA activities, helped students interrogate the multiple categories that structure people's identities, including gender and sexuality.

The Other Side is a picture book that explores the developing relationship between neighbor girls, one Black and one White, who have been told by their mothers to not cross the fence that separates their properties. This is not the only straight book that can be queered, of course, but Maree, Rose, and Jill all found it to be a compelling story and one that helped them to facilitate the kinds of conversations around identities that they valued. Additionally, since Jacqueline Woodson is an award-winning author, her books are accessible in many schools and libraries. This particular story centers on how these girls negotiate a relationship while navigating explicit and implicit rules regarding racialized boundaries and safety. The book clearly makes a statement about racial division, both historic and contemporary. It also, however, can be seen as a book about the desire for friendships between girls that are more allowed at some ages than others and about bending and breaking the rules of how someone is *supposed to be* if a particular identity is assigned to them. In other words, while the most salient interpretation of this book is one that centers on race, it can be a text that inspires thinking about the regulation of other identity categories as well.

BEGINNING DISCUSSIONS OF UNWRITTEN GENDER RULES

Maree's reading of *The Other Side* to her class the year she taught 3rd-grade was her first attempt at exploring queer elements of straight texts. She had noticed an increase in the number of put-downs she was hearing on the playground, including students calling each other "gay" and "girly," and wanted to use her teaching to address how language is used to devalue people. She'd already done other kinds of anti-bullying teaching, but she knew she needed to disrupt students' fixation on using the categories of gender and sexuality as a way to exclude and put down others. Maree's teaching in this lesson, as with others, centered on her read-aloud, although she had also planned discussion and writing activities to accompany it.

Reading Aloud in the Anchor Lesson

When it came time for the lesson, Maree explained that she had a new book to read to the class and that the reading would be followed by some group work to explore the themes in the story. Before reading, Maree showed her students the picture on the cover and they shared what they liked about it. Maree knew her students' needs and fixations well, because during the read-aloud they brought up questions about gender categories before she had the chance! While looking at the page Maree was reading, a student interrupted her to spontaneously ask, "That's a girl? It looks like a boy!" Without a single word from Maree, the idea of gender norms and who fits them was up for discussion, but Maree wanted to read more of the book before this discussion got any deeper, so she continued reading.

One of the first places Maree stopped her reading was when she paused to ask, "What is Mama talking about when she says, 'That's the way things have always been'?" After hearing some of the students' ideas, Maree pushed their thinking a little more. What, she asked students, might they "always do" even if no one ever said it is what they *had* to do? Are rules always written down? How do we even know when something is a rule? Students decided that outside of things like official laws, repeatedly enacting routines were the main way that ideas became solidified as rules; doing the same thing over and over created expectations that created rules. Through this conversation, Maree repeatedly drew her students' attention to how categories come to be and how rules, even informal ones that we don't *have* to follow, shape what we do and who we are.

Extending the Anchor Lesson

After reading, Maree divided the students into small groups to discuss what she called "the things we do every day that we don't really think so much about." She asked them to use the book and their own lives as their guide. Each group received a question to focus their work, such as one of the following:

- How do we know what are girl things and what are boy things?
- What's a boy book and what's a girl book? How do you know?
- What does it mean to act like a boy or girl?
- Can a man be a kindergarten teacher? Why or why not?

Maree gave each student a marker and they worked together to take notes on pages of construction paper on their tables.

During these discussions, her students uncovered many of gender's unwritten rules in their daily lives. Most boys seemed clear initially on the kinds of books, toys, colors, and other items that were "boy things" and "girl things" or "boy books" and "girl books." They started listing ideas right away with little hesitation or doubt. Boy things for them included the colors black and green, video games, action-packed comics, physical strength, and *The Dangerous Book for Boys* (Iggulden & Iggulden, 2007). Girl things they named included skirts, makeup, and *The Daring Book for Girls* (Buchanan & Peskowitz, 2009). Several girls, however, interrupted the boys when their gendered assumptions did not apply to the girls' own lives. For example, one male student suggested that videogames were boy things because "girls don't like to play them," but a girl in the group indignantly responded, "What?!" and shared that she really liked video games. When clothes were discussed, one of the girls said, "I rarely wear skirts!" Through the discussions, some boys also noticed where their ideas about these categories were inaccurate or incomplete. For example, after being challenged by the girls in his group about their interest in video games, one boy conceded that gender is more complex. He said, "Well, actually, there are no boy colors or boy or girl anythings!" With input from both girls and boys, students continued to modify their ideas, eventually suggesting that things are "considered" boy things and girl things. In this way, they were learning to question categories and "the way things have always been" with regard to gender by highlighting the artificial nature of unwritten gender expectations and expanding what is possible for people assigned to these categories.

Questioning categories of gender by reflecting on the unwritten rules that guide people's behavior created space for students to understand the interrelated categories of the heterosexual matrix in new and more expansive (if not always accurate) ways (Ryan, Patraw, & Bednar, 2013). For example, as one small group was discussing children's traditionally gendered behavior, a student claimed that "when a boy acts like a girl and dresses up like a girl, he's gay." Other students in the group agreed that being gay meant "when a boy acted like a girl or a girl acted like a boy." This led a student to share how he'd seen an example of a gay person on a television show, where, in his words, "a guy was wearing lip gloss, earrings, a skirt, and got plastic surgery." Other students offered stories of children they knew at school whose gender expression didn't always align with the gender they'd been assigned at birth. While their terminology and definitions weren't always accurate or appropriate, this process of questioning gender categories helped students recognize the connection between categories of gender expression and sexuality. They understood that transgressing one of the matrix categories could disrupt others.

While this conversation suggests that students were lacking a deeper understanding and a vocabulary to describe LGBTQ people and topics, they did not lack the knowledge about their existence. We see in these examples how students move from discussions of traditional gender roles and expressions to an expansion of those ideas, to explorations of gender nonconformity, to the recognition of people whose gender identities might not be the same as their gender assigned at birth. While many of these conversations were still marked by misperceptions and surface-level understandings, they provided a space for students' vast knowledge about gender rules—gained from their own experiences, from the experiences of people around them, and from popular culture—to be voiced and sometimes even challenged and expanded.

Students' confidence to explore these ideas might have come at least in part from Maree's approach to the activity. At many points in the lesson, she assured the students that there were no right or wrong answers and that the purpose was simply "to listen and share." This encouraged students to reflect on and share their views and experiences without the fear of being told they were incorrect. Yet it was the students' own experiences with gender that, when given some tools and encouragement, provided the impetus for their in-depth conversations that questioned social and cultural categories. The work the class did around this book shaped students' reading behaviors for the remainder of the school year. They frequently picked up LGBTQ-themed books and had conversations about the characters. They developed a language about gender and sexuality that challenged the ways that they'd used words like "girly" and "gay" in the past.

STOP AND THINK

- Do your students use put-downs related to gender and sexuality? How could you address those in class to help students expand the boundaries of those categories?
- How could lessons like this one go farther to break down the gender binary of "boys" and "girls"? How do we help students recognize the stereotypes in our culture related to this binary while still working to move beyond them?

ANCHOR LESSONS AS TOUCHSTONES FOR CONTINUED LEARNING

As in Maree's anchor lesson, *The Other Side* also helped Rose and Jill's 4th/5th-grade students develop a queer lens. Early in the school year, Rose and Jill used this reading and an exploration of "the way things have always been" as a touchstone experience for their class to shape how children thought about identity and power. Where Maree used this text to help with bullying around gender and sexuality on the playground, the idea for the lesson in this class grew from teaching that Rose and Jill had done to explore the unequal power in binary categories of identity such as race, age, ability, and socioeconomic class (Hermann-Wilmarth et al., 2017). Rose had already read Mildred Taylor's (1987) *The Friendship* aloud to the class, so students had started thinking about how race matters with regard to relationships. In her reading of *The Other Side*, Jill wanted to help students think about how gender and expectations around gender also inform the kinds of relationships that people are "allowed" to have and what kinds of expectations, written and unwritten, are present for people within different gender categories. The teachers hoped this lesson would build on students' prior knowledge of identity from these lessons while providing an opportunity to get more specific about how the categories of gender and sexuality are constructed. Jill saw her role as that of a facilitator who could support student responses if they queered the story; however, she did not want to force her ideas into the discussion. She and Rose, who was participating and observing, but not the lead teacher for this text, were prepared to follow the students' lead as they took up her questions.

What This Looked Like

Once the 4th/5th-graders were gathered on the carpet, Jill showed the cover of the book to the students and read the author's letter at the beginning of the text that frames the story as a call to tear down fences. As a class, they thought about fences, real and imaginary, in their town before beginning the story. Jill paused a few pages in after reading, "That summer everyone and everything on the other side of that fence seemed far away. When I asked my mama why, she said, 'Because that's the way things have always been.'" Looking up from the book, Jill invited students into a discussion by asking "What does that mean, 'the way things have always been?'" Students immediately drew on their knowledge of a variety of identity categories, and race in particular, to understand the text:

> *Beatrice:* That slavery and racism has been going on for over 300 years, so she's probably thinking that. Like it has just always been that way. Her mom grew up like that, and now she's growing up like that, and now it is just repeating.
>
> *Jill:* What other things have just always been?
>
> *Jonah:* The N-word has just always been there.
>
> *Jill:* Okay, it's always been a part of the language you've heard? Okay. Other things?
>
> *Alice:* Um, like, like separation has always been there.
>
> *Jill:* Interesting. Separation between whom?
>
> *Alice:* Between people, like, that are different. Like people of color and White people. Like boys and girls. Like adults and kids. Like a lot. There's just a lot of separation from people.
>
> *Jill:* So, people who fit into different identity categories have been separated from each other for a long time?
>
> *Alice:* Yeah.

As students continued to discuss the story, they made connections to other books where characters were seen as different, referring to a broad spectrum of identities. To direct their focus, Jill reminded the students of their discussion of binary categories, and asked them about what divides groups of people. Almost in unison, the class responded, "*Power!*" Jill nodded. "Let's keep this in mind as we keep reading."

While this was a good discussion, it was not the discussion Jill had planned or hoped for because gender categories had barely been mentioned, let alone questioned. She looked at Rose at one point and shrugged as if to say, "Well, okay! This is important, but we'll have to plan something else to help us queer a text." Jill had assumed that, like Maree's class, the 4th/5th-graders would make a seamless jump to ideas around bodies and gender, and just like that, students would question these categories and this straight text would be queered. But, like all teaching, it was not neat and easy, and Jill knew that pushing students into the thinking that she wanted them to do would be less fruitful in the long run than following their lead.

Furthermore, the discussions students were having around identities and power were in keeping with the work of the class and were ideas that Jill and Rose hoped that students would engage with that school year. As she turned the page of the book to continue reading, she resigned herself to finding another book that might help the class more deeply explore topics of gender and sexuality.

But as the story progressed and Annie and Clover's friendship developed, the students' focus began to shift. The first part of this shift happened when students questioned the power of rules. This discussion was an important step toward students' ability to question categories because it allowed students to reflect on the power behind the formation and regulation of categories and the ways they are maintained.

Students' gasped upon seeing an illustration of Annie and Clover holding hands as Annie helped Clover climb the fence. "She's gonna get in trouble." Alecia intoned. "Why?" Jill wondered. "The rule," Alecia replied. Students discussed who makes rules, why, and which, if any, deserve to be broken. Students drew on their knowledge of race and age and power to consider how rules worked and how "rules that don't have a purpose that you can see" are bad, but "laws so you don't get hurt . . . to make things fair-ish" are good. Students wondered if the girls touching each other as they held hands was breaking a rule since, as Molly pointed out, it felt like something their moms probably wouldn't like. In this moment, Molly, Alice, and Seth put their recognition of how unwritten rules can create trouble into words. While we cannot be sure if the rule-breaking they were concerned about was regarding a Black and White child holding hands, two girls holding hands, or both, they clearly felt that whatever was happening, "their parents wouldn't like it."

Students continued to shift toward questioning categories of the heterosexual matrix as the book came to a close. The story ended with the lines "'Someday somebody's going to come along and knock this old fence down,' Annie said. And I nodded. 'Yeah,' I said. 'Someday.'" When Jill and Rose asked, "What fences do we need to knock down?" Alice immediately responded, "Fences between the races, and fences between boys and girls." Now that a student was inviting the class to consider the category of gender, Jill immediately took her up on it, encouraging students to not just notice this binary but trouble and expand it. Jasmine said:

> Well, boys and girls have different kinds of power. Because, like, I know that when a boy does a thing that is seen as a 'girl thing,' he gets in trouble. People make fun of him. And a girl can just do that thing *because she's a girl*! And girls don't get in as much trouble if they do a thing that most people think is a boy thing! Like . . . what people wear. Girls can wear pants but boys can't wear dresses.

Jill pushed Jasmine to clarify even more. "Why not? What would happen if a boy did wear a dress?" Doug stepped in. "Bullies are violent to them." Pushing again, Jill asked, "Why?" Doug responded, "Because they are breaking a rule about being boys and that isn't really allowed." His words brought together the ideas of gender, unwritten rules, and power. They demonstrate his developing queer lens and ability to question categories. Like Clover and Annie, whose friendship wasn't really allowed, Doug drew on Jasmine's and Alice's thoughts to conclude that boys doing "girl things" also isn't allowed. This reading and talk served as a touchstone for future learning. The thinking they did during *The Other Side* helped students develop a queer lens that they could and would deploy when questioning LGBTQ and other identity categories as the school year progressed.

Ripples Over Time

Two days later, Molly showed Jill her response to the homework prompting students to draw a picture that depicted "the way things have always been," inspired by Annie and Clover. "This is a girl wearing a skirt and then this is a picture of a girl wearing pants. Like, sometimes that can be hard for girls? Like in the picture in the book, the girls are wearing dresses. And that is how things have always been." Alice also drew images of girls doing traditionally "girly" things (baking) and not so traditionally "girly" things (playing football). "I like both," she reported. Molly and Alice both drew images that questioned the category of gender as the class finished reading *The Other Side* and moved on to other books. But, this questioning of categories did not end there.

Three weeks later, inspired by the reading of *Each Kindness* (Woodson, 2012), Rose was leading a lesson about how to be an ally to people who are experiencing discrimination based on their identities. Alice raised her hand after the class watched a video showing how a White woman stood up for a Black woman in the grocery store (S. Butler, 2012). "This is like *The Other Side*. It's the way things have always been. The clerk made assumptions about the Black woman because they are different." This reminder to question taken-for-granted ways of being became part of Alice's role in the class. Even months later, Alice made this connection to information about bathrooms, transphobia, and the need for terms such as "gender assigned at birth." She recognized that the limiting gender binary had such power because it was "just the way things have always been. That's why transgender people are hard for some people to understand." The ripples from reading and discussing *The Other Side* in ways that questioned categories continued to spread.

While *The Other Side* lesson took only one afternoon, it served as a foundational experience for the class, and was instrumental in developing students' abilities to question categories. Because of the conversations around race and gender categories during the reading of *The Other Side*, students had a language and a lens for thinking about multiple identities, including LGBTQ identities, and why those identities are often treated in discriminatory ways. For both Maree's 3rd-grade class and Rose's 4th/5th-grade class, once the content of these anchor lessons became a regular part of classroom discourse, they facilitated new ways of thinking for students and teachers that helped them question and discuss taken-for-granted and culturally constructed notions of identity categories over time.

USING THIS METHOD WITH ANOTHER ANCHOR TEXT

For teachers who aren't able to bring texts with LGBTQ representations into their classrooms for myriad reasons, the process of queering books like *The Other Side* can, as we've shown, open a window for students to question taken-for-granted ideas that, in fact, might be the very reasons for this censorship of identity in the first place. After seeing this example, let's think about the books you already have on your shelf that might offer possibilities for your own work. In addition to the example below, we've also included other books that might help you do this in the Appendix.

We have written elsewhere (Hermann-Wilmarth & Ryan, 2015a; Ryan & Hermann-Wilmarth, 2013) about queering straight texts, and believe that such opportunities arise fairly commonly in many of the books regularly read as a part of elementary ELA. Consider, for example, Despereaux, the mouse in DiCamillo's (2003) *The Tale of Despereaux*. In this Newbery Award–winning book, Despereaux Tilling is a mouse who never fits in with those around him. He is smaller than he is supposed to be, he enjoys *reading* books rather than *eating* them, and he falls in love with a human instead of with another mouse. Despereaux's family disapproves of him in multiple ways, but they especially disapprove of this love. Not only does Despereaux's body not match the size of other male mice, but he does not enjoy the activities that define who mice are supposed to be. All of these parts of him are considered wrong. Despereaux's very being makes those around him question the categories that his family and community operate by.

Therefore, teachers' anchor lessons with this text can focus on how Despereaux's ability to stay true to who he is ends up breaking various rules. As the class reads more and more of the book, students could keep a running list of the ways that Despereaux's behaviors transgress the ideas of his family and community. These can then be compared to the rules that students navigate in their own lives. Teachers can use those lists and discussions as opportunities to draw direct parallels to rules and experiences around gender and sexuality. They could ask questions such as these: What activities are and are not allowed for boys and girls? What happens when people break the rules that are supposed to define who they are? How are people who don't look like we expect them to look stereotyped? How are they treated? What do we know about families who disapprove of their children? What kinds of relationships are forbidden and which ones are encouraged? How does this shape how people are allowed to exist in the world in safe ways? These kinds of questions can help students connect Despereaux's experiences with things students know from their own lives and help them question the categories around bodies, gender, and love that exist in the real world.

STOP AND THINK

- What books can you think of right now that have characters who queer the identity categories that they or others claim for them?
- Consider any of the following characters, and identify ways that they queer identity categories through their bodies, genders, and what/who they love:
  - ✓ Harry Potter and Hermione Granger in J. K. Rowling's series
  - ✓ Jess and Leslie in *Bridge to Terabithia* (Patterson, 1977)
  - ✓ Gerald the Giraffe in *Giraffes Can't Dance* (Andreae, 2001)
  - ✓ Red Crayon in *Red: A Crayon's Story* (Hall, 2015)
  - ✓ Oliver in *Oliver Button Is a Sissy* (dePaola, 1979)
  - ✓ Max in *Where the Wild Things Are* (Sendak, 1963)

Part III

QUESTIONING SILENCES IN EXPANDED REPRESENTATIONS

I think "Princess Boy" was sweet and I think [Dyson] wasn't afraid to be himself and that's just like Joe from "Totally Joe" because he isn't afraid to be himself and his heart is telling him to be different and both Dyson and Joe are following their heart. Everyone is different in their own way and they have very similar brains and hearts even though they are very different people. I think Dyson's family is really brave because his family has supported him all this way and that is one nice family!

—Anna, 5th-grader

In this reflective writing-for-thinking activity, Anna, one of Maree's students, demonstrates her ability to compare and contrast aspects of characters, plot points, and major themes from two texts. One of the books she's writing about, a novel called *Totally Joe* (Howe, 2005) that we wrote about in Chapter 3, expands representations to include LGBTQ people, since the book's protagonist is Joe, who is a White gay male. The other book she is writing about, a picture book called *My Princess Boy* (Kilodavis, 2009), helps readers question categories of how boys "should" act by telling the story of Dyson, a young African American boy who wants to wear dresses. In her writing, Anna is able to think through and beyond these differences. She recognizes how these characters aren't the same but instead are both "different in their own way." By bringing these two books together and asking Anna to think through the points of similarity and differences, Maree is helping her use the new approach we outline here in Part III: Questioning Silences in Expanded Representations. In this approach, we combine the expanding representations and questioning categories approaches. Specifically, we look at how questioning categories through a queer lens (discussed in Part II) can be applied to expanding representations (discussed in Part I). In other words, how can we complicate students' understandings of LGBTQ identities beyond the representations offered in texts included for elementary school readers? How can we help students think beyond the binary of expanding representations *or* questioning categories to understand that even books *with* LGBTQ characters in them can be queered?

Central to the questioning representations approach are theories about intersectional identities (Crenshaw, 1991) and "single story" representations (Adichie, 2009) that draw attention to the multiple layers of who we are. After all, as the poet Audre Lorde (1984) said, "We do not live single issue lives" (p. 138). These theories draw attention to that and help complicate notions that there is only one way to be LGBTQ. By layering different characters and experiences, this third approach can help disrupt assumptions about the LGBTQ community and highlight the diversity within it.

The two chapters in Part III each examine a different method of teaching. In Chapter 6 we consider how text sets can help to address gaps in the types of LGBTQ representations typically available in children's books, particularly those involving people of color, poor people, and people with diverse gender expressions and with other minoritized identities (Hermann-Wilmarth & Ryan, 2016; see also ccbc.education. wisc.edu/books/pcstats.asp). Text sets, we argue, provide a way for characters from different texts to complicate each other's representations. We saw this in the example of Anna's writing that opened this part where a gender creative person of color and a gay White male character who exist in different texts create deeper understanding for Anna as a reader. In Chapter 7 we look at how a whole unit, anchored by the close study of a novel that expands LGBTQ representations across race, class, and gender expression, offers possibilities for creating nuance and expanded representations that more accurately show the diversity of LGBTQ people's lives.

CHAPTER 6

Acknowledging Silences in LGBTQ Inclusion

There's an old folktale from India called "The Blind Men and the Elephant." In this story, six blind men are asked to describe what an elephant is like. Each one touches just one part of the elephant and uses that information to make his inference. The catch is that each man touched a different part of the elephant, giving six different interpretations. One man, for example, touches the trunk and claims the elephant is like a snake. Another touches the elephant's side and suggests an elephant is like a wall. A third touches the elephant's tusk and decides an elephant is like a spear, and so on. More traditional interpretations of this story sometimes suggest the blind men are foolish for not reaching a different conclusion. We, however, think it's important to notice that each man's individual understanding is accurate based on the information he had access to. It wasn't the men's abilities of observation or interpretation but rather the fact that they each only had access to one point of data and no one provided them with any additional access that kept them from building a more precise, holistic picture.

This can also be the danger when it comes to the representations we include in our classrooms. We hope it's clear from Part I that we value expanding representations to include LGBTQ people, even if it's just in one book or one lesson. We truly believe that such actions send important messages to all your students about the value of LGBTQ lives and make your classroom a more inclusive place. However, we also recognize that providing students with single or limited representations can be like giving the blind men access to just one part of the elephant. No single representation can possibly come close to covering the nuances of a whole community of people, so we have to be careful not to suggest to students that it does. Likewise, even when teachers include multiple representations of LGBTQ people, following the expanding representations method, if they don't intentionally ask students to notice how each of those representations calls into question what they know about the identity category itself, there is the possibility that cultural ideas about LGBTQ people will be reified. In other words, as inclusive teachers we want to move away from asking simply *if* LGBTQ people are represented and instead turn our

attention more specifically to *how* they are represented and what the overall message is to students as a result of those representations. We want
students to consider this nuance, and we believe that ELA practices can
help. When teachers ask students to do this, students' worldviews can be
expanded. They see more possibilities for who other people are and for
who they might become. They have the opportunity to understand that
identity categories are always changing and that similarly labeled people
have wide ranging experiences.

For those reasons, this chapter will suggest ways teachers can simultaneously draw on both expanding representations and questioning categories.
The combined approach we describe here can help teachers include even
limited representations in our classrooms to support windows and mirrors
of LGBTQ identities while still critiquing and expanding them. It means
that even when representations are present, readers should pay attention
to the systems that created those identities in the first place. When teachers
are able to take this combined approach, their students benefit from both
the inclusion of LGBTQ representations and the simultaneous analysis of
gender, sexuality, and other layers of identity in all characters and texts.
Besides helping students have a more accurate and nuanced view of diverse
identities, this approach develops students' critical thinking. When students
can not only see representations of LGBTQ people but also understand how
systems work with regard to multiple and intersecting identities, they are
more prepared to be participants in a multicultural world.

THE IMPORTANCE OF COMPLICATING
"SINGLE STORY" REPRESENTATIONS

As a teacher, have you ever created a text set around a topic? You knew that
just one book about a subject as complex as the Civil War or rainforests or
our solar system wasn't enough to teach students all that you wanted them
to learn, so you gathered a variety of different texts, perhaps from different
genres or including a variety of perspectives. You probably thought about
the ways that introducing students to these different books might continue
to deepen students' understanding of the topic you were studying.

This sense of needing more complete information about a topic is at
the heart of novelist Chimamanda Adichie's (2009) theory about the danger of what she calls a "single story." Adichie explains that *single stories*
are times when we repeatedly see an event or a group of people portrayed
in only one way. Picture, for example, what you think of when you hear
"scientist." Are you thinking of a White man in a lab coat holding some
kind of chemical in a test tube or beaker? That's the picture many of us
have been given over and over in our society until the point that, for many

people, such an image creates a single story of who scientists are and what they do. As a woman from Nigeria who came to college in the United States, Adichie talks about encountering many Americans' single stories about Nigeria specifically and Africa more generally. In turn, she also had to face the single stories she had of Americans. Of course there are, in reality, many White male scientists who wear lab coats and work with chemicals in beakers. Similarly, some of the ideas Americans had about Nigerians and that Adichie had about Americans were at least partially true for some places or some people. The problem with these and other single stories, Adichie argues, is not that they are necessarily untrue, but that they are *incomplete*. There are scientists that fit our stereotypical image, but there are also lots of other scientists who look other ways and do other kinds of things. There are over 50 countries in Africa with different kinds of climates and cultures filled with cities and suburbs and rural areas. Some Americans live like characters on *Gilmore Girls* or *The Wire* or *The Real Housewives* reality shows, but many others do not. In each of these cases, the pictures people have in their minds cover only one particular slice of a much more complex real world. Working to interrupt single stories, therefore, isn't about proving the single story wrong as much as it is about continually troubling, complicating, and layering individual representations so that the single story does not stand in for and mask the intricacy of the many other stories that are not heard.

To help disrupt single stories related to identity categories, an intersectional perspective is useful. This perspective holds that all people have multiple and layered identities (Kumashiro, 2002) and that the experience of one identity held by a person informs how the other identities held by that same person are lived (Crenshaw, 1991). In other words, people are never just one part of themselves at a time. We (the authors), for example, aren't *just* women. We're also White and middle-class and lesbians and cisgender and able-bodied. That combination of identities matters to how we live in the world. It means we will likely have some different life experiences than straight women of color or working-class White lesbians or disabled transgender women might. Being women might connect all of us and our experiences in particular ways, but our other identities shape how we live out being a woman in ways we might not share. For another example, because a person of color who is also poor and LGBTQ-identified experiences the world through three traditionally marginalized identities, this intersection of oppressions complicates their access to opportunities in multiple ways. Unfortunately, people's lived realities of such layered marginalizations are often the very stories that are underrepresented (Cohen, 1997; Crenshaw, 1991). When we think about intersectionality in our classrooms and ELA teaching, we look for ways to recognize and represent the stories of people whose identities are layered in these multiply marginalized ways.

DOING THE WORK OF QUESTIONING REPRESENTATIONS

What do these ideas mean for you and your teaching as it relates to LGBTQ topics? The first thing to remember is that the LGBTQ community is extremely diverse. If you've ever gone to or seen pictures of a Pride parade, you may have noticed the sheer variety of people involved in the community. There are gay men and lesbian women celebrating their sexual orientations. There are transgender people—who may also identify as men, women, genderqueer, or nonbinary—celebrating their gender identities and gender expressions. Some are young, some are old. Some are White, some are people of color. Some are poor, some are rich. Some use wheelchairs or are Deaf while others are able-bodied and/or hearing. Some are club goers, some belong to religious groups, and some are both! Many are part of several of these categories all at once. The diversity of the larger world is reflected in the LGBTQ community.

When it comes to characters in children's books or other curricular materials, however, representations of LGBTQ people are almost always White, middle-class, able-bodied, and cisgender (Hermann-Wilmarth & Ryan, 2016; Lester, 2014; Young, 2015). They're also frequently adults who are partnered or married. Therefore, even when children do get to read LGBTQ-inclusive books, they can get a skewed sense of who LGBTQ people are because the pages of these books don't contain the more diverse realities of many LGBTQ people's actual lives.

The work we suggest teachers can do here is to diversify representations through text sets in ways that help students visualize and question the intersectionality of identities represented across the titles. In this way, students see multiple, varied representations of LGBTQ people. As Maree's 3rd-graders realized when discussing "girl things" and "boy things" in Chapter 5, classifications that initially seem strict can stretch and fall apart in the face of diversity. Therefore, layering LGBTQ representations can help readers understand the messy, expansive nature of these identity categories. In other words, with a teacher's help students can learn to notice how identity categories work, not just in books with straight characters, as we explored in Part II, but also in LGBTQ-inclusive texts. This approach means drawing students' attention to questioning and expanding the categories of the heterosexual matrix—biological sex, gender, and sexuality—while also layering ideas about race, class, ability, religion, and other categories that shape how we live in the world.

Building a Text Set Around Diverse Gender Creative and Transgender Youth

As you read about in Chapter 3, Maree decided to include LGBTQ characters in her ELA teaching by reading *Totally Joe* (Howe, 2005) aloud to her 4th-graders. Including this gay character's voice in the classroom helped students think about his experiences. It also helped them question gender categories, because in addition to being gay, Joe expresses his gender in several gender creative and nonconforming ways. For example, he tells the reader about dressing up in his mother's clothes as a child and how he liked to play with Barbie dolls. Using Joe's lists about what makes a "guy guy" and another character's comments about how dressing up is "kinda gay," Maree and her students questioned the rigidity of categories with regard to gender and sexuality. Layering different ways of living these categories was possible in this text because Joe is not the only gay character in the book, but he is the least stereotypically masculine. This helped Maree and her students begin to disrupt the single story of who LGBTQ people are and how they behave.

In addition to the multiple gay characters in *Totally Joe*, stories that students and Maree shared during their discussions of this text also helped layer additional perspectives of LGBTQ people, including transgender people. For example, when students feared that one character's parents would disown him for being gay, Maree shared a story about one of her friends who was disowned when they came out as transgender (Ryan, Patraw, & Bednar, 2013). Since this was the first time the class had discussed what *transgender* means, Maree explained that some transgender people "feel as though they were born in the wrong bodies." Drawing on the close friendships she has with several transgender people, Maree outlined a range of ways a person might transition—a process, she explained, that meant moving toward living authentically as who they really are. These ways included "by how they live their lives," "by taking hormones which change some of their outsides," or "by surgery." A few students were confused or uncomfortable ("That's weird!"), but others had stories from their own families and experiences with popular culture that they were able to share. One student said, "I know someone. He used to be a girl, and he took the hormones that you were talking about, and now he's a boy. Like everybody, like he . . . well, he's really nice."

Although reading *Totally Joe* sparked discussions about the experiences of transgender people, that text did not contain any transgender characters that students could get to know. Maree also recognized that *Totally Joe* didn't address other kinds of diversity, especially related to race, and that her students needed additional information and support to understand the experiences of transgender people in greater depth. In response to these needs, Maree created a text set of materials that could accompany her read-aloud of *Totally Joe*. While still not representing the full range of LGBTQ diversity, these additional texts, including both picture books and short videos, helped Maree layer additional LGBTQ voices and perspectives into her ELA curriculum, including transgender people's experiences and diverse representations of race when possible.

Exploring Gender Expression: Seeing It in Practice. The first text Maree shared was a video clip of an African American family with a gender creative child being interviewed on a popular morning news program. Before showing the clip, Maree explained that after their discussions related to *Totally Joe* regarding gender stereotypes, gender expression, and gender identity, she'd thought about a family she'd seen on television. This family had a little boy who doesn't identify as a girl but who likes to wear girls' clothes. In fact, his parents, Cheryl and Dean Kilodavis, referred to their son, Dyson, as a "princess boy" because he is happiest wearing pink dresses. Before showing the clip, Maree told students that they were going to watch an interview with this boy and his mother (Bell, 2011) and, while they were watching, they should think about what they noticed and how it relates to *Totally Joe*.

When the video was over, she sent students back to their seats to do some free writing about that topic using a page she'd created with the prompt at the top. After time to write, she gathered them back on the carpet to continue their discussion. Maree opened the conversation by sharing things she'd noticed about the video, thereby modeling the kinds of thinking that students might do. The first thing she mentioned was Dyson's mother's initial discomfort at seeing Dyson in girls' clothes, "probably because of our preconceived notions about what boys and girls should do and wear." Maree said this reminded her about discussions they'd had about gender while reading *Totally Joe*. The second thing she brought up was how the psychologist interviewed in the clip said "we need to recognize that there is more than one way to be a boy, and more than one way to be a girl," which, Maree said, "gave her some things to think about." The third thing she highlighted for the class was their talk about the need for parents to love their children for who they are, which reminded her of a few places in *Totally Joe*. "Like Colin and his dad!" a student responded, referencing the character of Joe's boyfriend whose father demonstrates discomfort around gay people. "Exactly," Maree said. She remarked on how Dyson's other family members, including his dad and his brother, encouraged Dyson to be himself so he would be happy and healthy. And finally, she closed by highlighting the ways that Dyson's full school staff had "rallied around" the family and decided to support their choices, especially when it came to Dyson being Cinderella for Halloween. After modeling her thinking in this way, Maree turned the floor back over to the students by saying, "So those are some of my reflections. Now I'd love to hear from you. What are *your* thoughts? What stood out to you?"

The writing that students shared showed empathy, engagement with both texts, and a sophisticated sense of text-to-self and text-to-text connections. Students' perspectives varied, but many traced connections between Dyson and Joe, particularly related to the two characters' creative expressions of gender and their families' positive reactions. For example, Spark wrote: "Dyson wasn't afraid to be himself and his family supported and loved him anyway. Dyson just liked pretty things and there wasn't anything wrong with him. Joe is also not afraid to be himself and his parents let him be whoever he wants to be." Phil wrote, "I think that the video was good because it let kids know that girls' clothes are not just for girls. It relates to the story because Dyson just wants to be who he is. They [Dyson and Joe] are both free." Imani wondered about how these boys' gender expressions could influence what people might assume about their sexuality. She wrote:

> My thoughts about the video Princess Boy are how did the mother handle other people thinking, "why is she letting him dress like that?" Because I would not. This story is related to the story Totally Joe because Joe and Colin dressed up [for Halloween] as Bert and Ernie from Sesame Street and Colin's dad said that that is gay, and Dyson dressed up as a princess so that might tell us that his dad might think that he is gay too.

Sierra also made connections between diverse characters. While Dyson and Joe have different identities, they experience similar negativity from people around them because of their gender nonconforming behavior, although she inaccurately grouped that behavior under the umbrella of "being gay," which was not a part of Dyson's identity (see Figure 6.1). Sierra wrote:

> How I think these stories relate [is] because in the Princess Boy [video] Dyson was getting bullied just because he was gay. And in Totally Joe, Joe was getting bullied because he was gay. And really if you think about it really deeply, Dyson fits in Joe's shoes and the bullies that are bullying Dyson, they would fit into Kevin's shoes. So really the bullies are the same and the people getting picked on are really the same people.

Figure 6.1. Reflecting on *Totally Joe* and *My Princess Boy*

What are your thoughts about the video, *Princess Boy*? How does this relate to the story, <u>Totally Joe</u>?

> How I think these storys relate becaus in The Princess Boy Dyson was geting bullyed just because he was gay. And in Totally Joe, Joe was getting bullyed because he was gay. And really I if you think about it really deeply. Dyson fits in Joes Shoes and the bullys that are bullying Dyson, they would fit into Kevens Shoes. So really the bullys are the same and the people that are geting picked on, are really the same people.

Through this writing, students demonstrated their abilities to see both similarities and differences across two different representations of gender creative people, one a White, gay adolescent and the other a Black child. Sometimes, their hunt for these connections overlooked or conflated details that actually separated the characters, but these attempts showed an emerging ability to notice similarities among diverse characters while still recognizing at least some of their differences in identity. Bringing together these different texts helped Maree's students develop their ELA skills while simultaneously developing a deeper understanding of the diversity in and the connections across the LGBTQ community.

The exploration of intertextual connections across the LGBTQ community continued the next day when Maree read the book *My Princess Boy* that Dyson's mother had written about her son. Just as she had with *Totally Joe*, Maree began the lesson by reading the author's note to readers on the back cover, pausing to discuss words like "unconditional" and "compassion" in greater depth. When she asked the class whether they thought they had been learning about and practicing compassion through their work that year, the students agreed.

After reading, Maree wondered aloud why the illustrator only gave the characters in the book blank faces with no facial features drawn in. She prompted students to consider a connection between the people in *My Princess Boy* not having faces with the end of the book that says, "my princess boy is your princess boy," meaning this could be your child, or anyone's child. Students thought that made sense. They then connected that message to the life lesson in *Totally Joe* that says, "Life lesson for parents: love your kids. . . . And don't tell them 'people like that' make you uptight, because for all you know, your kids just might be 'people like that,' too" (Howe, 2005, p. 47). Students closed the discussion by sharing their thoughts on the main message of *My Princess Boy*. Indira said it was a message to be your own person. Violet said to accept someone no matter how different they seem. And Kyle said it is important to be who you are because it doesn't matter what other people think, only what you think.

Exploring Gender Identity: Seeing It in Practice.

Exploring Gender Identity: Seeing It in Practice. To continue to deepen these conversations, Maree added additional picture books to her text set: *10,000 Dresses* (Ewert, 2008) and *Be Who You Are* (Carr, 2010). Instead of focusing primarily on gender expression, as they had in *Totally Joe* and *My Princess Boy*, both of these new books featured transgender children assigned male at birth who identify as female. In *10,000 Dresses*, Bailey's family is not affirming of her gender identity; they refer to her with male pronouns and her brother threatens to kick her. In *Be Who You Are*, Hope's family is supportive of her gender identity; they respond encouragingly when she says she wants to use female pronouns.

Maree read *10,000 Dresses* first. Before reading, she showed students the cover of the book, as she usually did. Students were unsure if the child wearing a dress in the cover image was a boy or a girl. Maree shared the word *androgynous* with them, defining it as "when it isn't clearly distinguishable whether someone is male or female" because they "don't dress and present themselves so that you can tell." Maree then told the class that the main character was Bailey, who dreamed about dresses. A student pointed out that Bailey could be a boy or a girl's name. Maree asked students to compare and contrast *10,000 Dresses* with *My Princess Boy* as she read.

It quickly became clear that Bailey's transgender identity stretched students' understanding in new ways. For example, students noticed some people referred to Bailey as a boy while she referred to herself as a girl in her own thoughts. Maree asked them to share their ideas about why that might be. As Ashley explained, "The narrator kind of wants us to see her as a girl, because that's who Bailey feels she is." Alianna suggested: "It's like people . . . accept her if they call her a girl and they act like she's a girl because that's what she wants to be, she wants to be a girl." Indira followed up with more direct evidence, reminding the class that "Laurel called Bailey 'she' in the story because she accepts Bailey for who she is."

At this point in the conversation, Maree wrote "transgender" on the board. She reminded students they had talked about this term before while reading *Totally Joe* and asked students what they remembered about it. Kristen said it meant to change genders and that some people take medicine or have surgery to change their bodies. Spark said, "Sometimes people feel like they were born in the wrong body, so they make these changes so that their outsides match their insides." Megan said it meant "someone is a boy or a girl and they feel like they weren't meant to be that way, and then they would have to go back to the hospital and have surgery to change their body into what they want to be." Kyle reminded the class that "you don't have to have surgery . . . you can change your looks without having to have surgery." To bring these ideas together, Maree said that they were right, *transgender* meant "when you change your gender, or want to change your gender. You don't feel the way inside that you look and are on the outside."

Maree then brought their conversation about Bailey's transgender gender identity back into the context of the other texts they'd been reading. She asked the students to go back to their seats and complete a Venn diagram comparing and contrasting Bailey and Dyson. (See Alianna's writing example in Figure 6.2.) During their writing, students noted that Dyson was Black and Bailey was White, Dyson's parents and brother supported him and Bailey's didn't, and Dyson doesn't identify as female and Bailey does.

They also used pronouns to reflect these different gender identities. With only occasional exceptions, students referred to Dyson with male pronouns and Bailey with female pronouns as they wrote. Sometimes students struggled with these distinctions, coming up with constructions such as "[Bailey] feels like he is a girl." Students commonly wrote "both are boys" in the middle of their Venn diagrams, lacking any additional language to describe physical sex, but overall, students honored the characters' affirmed gender identities through their use of pronouns and other language.

Maree wrapped up the text set the next day with a quick read of *Be Who You Are*. This book confirmed the information students had learned throughout the rest of the text set. They noticed how Hope's situation was like Bailey's except that her family was supportive. It provided one additional representation and set of experiences for students to consider and

Figure 6.2. Venn Diagram Comparing *My Princess Boy* and *10,000 Dresses*

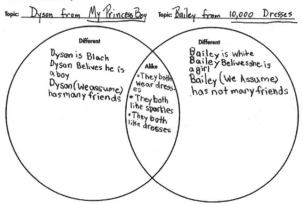

gave students another opportunity to practice using pronouns that matched people's identities.

Finding Familiar ELA Practices in This New Teaching

Through this set of texts, Maree drew on multiple books and a video to provide a variety of representations. As students worked with these texts, her students learned new vocabulary, engaged in reflective writing, compared and contrasted the traits of characters across books, made predictions about stories, thought carefully about pronouns and other uses of language, recognized text-to-text connections, used graphic organizers like Venn diagrams as prewriting activities, and made inferences about the themes of books based on both visual and textual evidence. Reading multiple texts, including a video, and thinking across them encouraged deep synthesis and critical thinking. Such synthesis even inspired some students to do free writing during their journal and free work time about the texts. Alianna wrote a piece entitled "Totally 10,000 Princess Boys" with a subtitle "A report on why it's good to be you." The report began, "Have you ever felt like you wanted to be like somebody else? Or have you ever tried being someone else just to 'fit in'? I know I have. So me, Joe, Bailey, and Dyson are going to show you how to be yourself and be happy."

These texts, therefore, with their various LGBTQ characters, did much more for students than just support their ELA learning. Reading about multiple characters who faced similar challenges emphasized the theme and even allowed students, like Alianna, to see themselves in relation to these experiences. In addition, seeing characters who had both overlapping and unique aspects of their identities helped interrupt a single story about LGBTQ people. Students could reflect on the different ways that LGBTQ people were represented and see how the community varies in terms of race,

---

STOP AND THINK

- What words that Maree used about gender identity, gender creativity, and transgender identities would you feel confident using in your teaching? What concepts would you want additional clarity on? Where could you go to find additional information?
- Maree's students are just starting to work with these topics. Do you have ideas for lessons that would push them into clearer understanding?
- In what ways could you help students look across these representations to question what they know about LGBTQ identities?

gender identity, and individual experiences. In these ways, the multiple representations they saw helped them simultaneously question categories and expand their experiences with representations of LGBTQ people.

CONSIDERATIONS AND CHALLENGES IN YOUR CONTEXT

Because this approach combines the previous two, it minimizes some of the risks inherent in trying each approach separately. For example, layering texts with various LGBTQ voices minimizes the risk of tokenism involved in portraying only a single representation or in portraying representations without consideration of the similarities and differences in the ways LGBTQ characters live out their identity labels. By giving attention to the ways categories are constructed in this approach, students can apply their queer lenses to the diversity of LGBTQ people. While the first approach does not necessarily limit teachers to including only one representation of LGBTQ identities, this approach pushes on that inclusion, inviting students to question those labels and create more nuanced understanding. Therefore, this third approach draws attention to how LGBTQ people are being represented and the consequences those representations have. Reading in this way allows students to notice and question the lack of diversity they may encounter in LGBTQ-inclusive books. This helps teachers move away from asking "should I teach this LGBTQ book" as a yes-or-no question and instead focus on possibilities for how a book could be taught or connected to other texts in ways that call into question silences and stereotypes.

However, this third approach doesn't avoid challenges completely. As with expanding representations, access to and the ability to use LGBTQ-inclusive books is not possible or safe for all teachers. Also, layering texts or deeply studying the multiple, intersecting identities in texts can take time. When teachers are already struggling to find time simply to read aloud at all, this kind of longer study might seem unlikely, yet even occasional opportunities to reflect on intersecting identity categories can be valuable. And finally, even though diversity in children's publishing is slowly increasing, diverse LGBTQ-inclusive characters and stories are still hard—if not impossible—to find. In Chapter 7 we share the teaching of Jacqueline Woodson's (2008) LGBTQ-inclusive book *After Tupac and D Foster,* which features African American characters, but such books remain extremely rare for elementary-school-age readers. Until there are more publishers willing to publish more diverse LGBTQ-inclusive books for this age group, we encourage teachers to use multiple forms of media, such as the video Maree showed or other multimedia texts. (See the Appendix for additional resource suggestions.) Streaming video sites like Vimeo and YouTube are platforms encouraging participatory cultures (Jenkins, 2006), which therefore may be more accessible to producers of diverse content and can connect teachers and students to a range of multimedia sources. Furthermore, the use of video and other multimodal text can increase student engagement (Willingham, 2009) and students' 21st-century skills such as transmediation (Harste, 2014; Jenkins, 2006; Siegel, 1995), especially when combined with print texts. While this solution comes with its own challenges regarding access to technology and Internet filters that allow LGBTQ content into schools, such additional sources of representation can be an important component in helping students learn about how the lives of LGBTQ people are as diverse as the lives of the rest of the world.

CHAPTER 7

Connecting LGBTQ Characters and the Larger World

Langston Hughes was gay? How did I not know this?

—Alice, 5th-Grader

At the end of the year, Rose's 4th/5th-graders were engaged in both a poetry unit and a study of the Flint, MI, water crisis which was at the time just becoming national news. She and Jill challenged students to make connections between these two subjects, including how identities might play a role in both the experience of the water crisis and the lenses through which poets write. During their study of Flint, the class had studied graphs about free and reduced-price lunch and average household income, as well as information about the racial demographics of the city, to help them get a sense of why the crisis was proving so difficult to escape and how having that much lead in the water could be considered environmental racism. As they studied poetry with the goal of writing poems in response to this crisis, they read work by Langston Hughes, Audre Lorde, and Jacqueline Woodson. While teaching the students about each poet, Rose and Jill asked students to consider what identity categories the poets shared. Intersectional identities with regard to race, class, and geography had been a clear focus of their year, so it was not surprising that students knew all three were African American, but they were startled when Jill said all three also belonged or belong to the LGBTQ community and wondered why they hadn't been taught that before. Rose replied, "We should think about why we don't often know if a person is gay or lesbian." She then asked them to think about how the experience of being both Black and gay may have changed over the decades that these poets wrote and lived. As Jill and Rose heard their students' surprise at the poets' LGBTQ identities, they decided to more explicitly layer discussions of sexuality into the identities they were already highlighting in their ELA curriculum. Those efforts are the focus of this chapter.

In Chapter 6 we saw how Maree created a text set of diverse transgender and gender creative characters to complicate the single story of the

LGBTQ community as White, gay, middle-class, and male, which was the representation students had seen in their novel study of *Totally Joe*. In this chapter, we will see how a group of students who looped with Rose in her multiage class (first as 4th-graders and then as 5th-graders) learned to question representations of LGBTQ people in ways that highlighted intersectional LGBTQ identities through a novel study of Jacqueline Woodson's *After Tupac and D Foster* (2008). To understand this text and the secondary character of Tash, who is Black, gay, and gender creative, students drew on their prior learning about both race and transgender topics as they began to think in more intersectional ways and learned more about the full diversity of LGBTQ people's lives.

TEACHING *AFTER TUPAC AND D FOSTER*

After Tupac and D Foster takes place in Queens, NY, in the mid-1990s and focuses on the friendship between two middle-school-age African American girls, Neeka and an unnamed narrator. Their friendship grows to include a third girl who calls herself D Foster and shows up in their neighborhood one summer afternoon. The three best friends spend much of their time hanging out in the neighborhood, talking about their experiences, listening to the music of Tupac Shakur, and contemplating their futures. Neeka has four brothers, two of whom are secondary characters: high school basketball star Jayjones, and gay, femme, church musician Tash, who is incarcerated for part of the novel. Tash disrupts popular single-story narratives that assume LGBTQ people are White and that all Black people are straight. Likewise, Tash is open and proud about his gender presentation, which is not stereotypically masculine. He is described lovingly by Neeka as "a true-blue sissy" (p. 59) and uses female terms to refer to himself.

    After Tupac was the first time Rose's students had read a book with a Black, gay, gender-nonconforming character, but reading other books with LGBTQ representations including *George* (Gino, 2015), *The Misfits* (Howe, 2001), and *Totally Joe* (Howe, 2005) prior to this text had helped them build a limited understanding of the LGBTQ community. For example, *Totally Joe* introduced students to a White, gay male protagonist and gay male secondary characters. *George* had reinforced that children can identify as LGBTQ and had built students' background knowledge specifically around transgender identities. While none of these books interrupted ideas that LGBTQ characters are White and middle-class, they provided the foundation Rose's students drew on when reading about Tash. In this way, reading and working with *After Tupac and D Foster* created space for students to rethink how both they and the larger culture in which they live situate gender expression, gayness, and Blackness.

Reading Aloud

When Rose and Jill decided to read this book with the 5th-graders in this multiage class, they knew that the wide-ranging topics—including scenes of incarceration, racial profiling by police, the role of the Black church, and the significance of Tupac's lyrics and life—would be more of a window than a mirror for most of the students, the majority of whom were White and middle-class. Through read-alouds, classroom discussions, independent research, writing prompts, and photographs, Rose and Jill helped the 5th-graders combine the limited background knowledge they had with information about current events to build a starting point for understanding the experiences of the characters in Woodson's text.

   Clarifying Terms and Topics. Reading this text started with Jill and the students discussing a basic question: "Does anyone know who Tupac was?" While most students did not, a few did. One student even knew about conspiracy theories suggesting Tupac was alive and where he was currently living. Drawing on this knowledge and references to other LGBTQ books they'd read in school such as *Totally Joe* (Howe, 2005), Jill and the 5th-graders wove a rich tapestry of connections and ideas to help them make meaning of Woodson's book. Jill found herself stopping to clarify moments in the text where intersectionality was highlighted. These discussions were wide-ranging. One time, Jill clarified what HIV is and the significance it carried during the time of the story. Another time, she and the students considered the differences between Jayjones's assertion that "brothers be hunted" (p. 69) after he was chased home by a cop and the narrator's commentary that "sisters were hunted too" (p. 70) to explain her vulnerability as a Black girl.

   One example of these discussions occurred when the students used their prior understanding of LGBTQ identities to question representations. Jill paused in her reading of a scene where family members were visiting Tash in prison. Students wondered if Tash might identify as transgender because Tash called himself a queen and referred to himself with other female terms. Students had learned about transgender people and the proper use of pronouns from *George,* but this was their first time encountering a gay-identified character who chose to use pronouns that didn't match their gender assigned at birth. When a classmate added, "I'm not sure. My brother is gay and he calls himself a girl, too," students had the opportunity to discuss multiple representations of gay, transgender, and gender-nonconforming people in a school setting where they knew these discussions were both welcome and important. Through these facilitated discussions, characters from multiple texts and people from students' real lives intermingled—Tash, Melissa, and students' own relatives—and students' notions of who LGBTQ people are and the language used within and outside the community was expanded and complicated. Likewise, students had the opportunity to consider identity in more nuanced ways. With just three examples—Tash, Melissa, and a student's brother—students were exposed to LGBTQ people who all occupy that identity differently. This kind of teaching helps students learn to develop a lens through which they can look at the world. This lens can help them see that identity is nuanced. People who claim the same identity labels live and experience that identity differently, and often that experience is reliant on the ways that multiple identities intersect. Encouraging such analysis can help students employ critical thinking both in and out of school.

Ideas that came up in discussion each day were extended through students' homework. For example, on the day discussed above, students responded to questions including: Is Tash like anyone you know? What would happen if there was a kid at school like Tash? How do you hope people would respond? Do people respond differently in a school community like this one than they do in our larger culture? Why or why not? The next day's reading then began with a discussion of students' writing. This gave students time to synthesize their own ideas with the understanding they'd gleaned from their peers.

Further Contextualizing of the Novel. Because Woodson's story is so nuanced and layered with the true complexities of a community, Jill did not want students to miss the richness it represents. Jill and the students kept a running list of major topics discussed in the book: overpolicing of people of color and incarceration rates among different racial groups, college and pro sports as a career option, hip-hop and rap music, foster care. One ongoing assignment during this unit was for students to select and research one or more of these topics. They found and read articles, wrote minireports, and shared what they learned with the group. Alecia, for example, researched the history of hip-hop. Her two-paragraph report, complete with a citation of the articles she had used, concluded with a list of the oppressions experienced by African Americans that had inspired the hip-hop movement and culture. In her presentation, she was able to connect information she'd just learned, such as the realities of police brutality, to central themes in *After Tupac and D Foster*. But, she realized, Woodson's characters had mentioned an additional element about hip-hop culture that hadn't come up in her research. Neeka, the narrator, and Jayjones had talked about the homophobia in some hip-hop, specifically how "Pac's lyrics ain't always cute when it comes to people like Tash" (Woodson, 2009, p. 58). "But," Alecia said, "nobody [in my research] talked about hip-hop people not liking gay people." Alecia pointed to the complexity—the intersectionality—present in Woodson's text. Alecia's research layered upon Woodson's text helped to interrupt single-story narratives about hip-hop. She and her classmates were learning to be attuned to both the importance of hip-hop to the African American community and to how hip-hop could be hostile to people with LGBTQ identities. Furthermore, they were learning to reflect on the tension of what it must be like to be Tash and to fit into both of those categories.

This process of reading, discussing, writing, and researching drove Jill and the students through the text and helped to structure their learning. Students had opportunities to puzzle out their understandings of what was happening in the text and make connections to other books they'd read as well as to current events.

Activities to Highlight Multiple Perspectives

To help students better understand the ways that identity matters in the lives of people, Jill created an image walk for the students as they neared the end of the book. At each table around the classroom, she placed an image that was connected to a topic raised in the book that students had been researching. Each image was numbered. Next to each image were strips of paper that gave students characters or roles to assume as they looked at the picture. They were asked to write a response to each picture from that perspective. Below is a sample of what the pictures depicted (in bold), and the perspectives to be taken while looking at the pictures:

Pride Parade

> You are Tash.
> You are one of the church ladies.
> You are Tash's mama, Miss Irene.
> You are your own parents.

Prancing Elites *[a predominantly African American dance team made up of members who are gay or gender nonconforming]*

> You are the narrator.
> You are Tupac.
> You are the neighborhood men playing chess who laughed at Tash.
> You are one of Neeka's little brothers.
> You are Miss Irene.

Black Lives Matter Protest

> You are Jayjones.
> You are the police officer who chased Jayjones.
> You are Neeka.
> You are the narrator.
> You are you.

Crumbling Steps of an Urban Brown Stone

You are D.

You are Neeka.

You are Miss Irene.

You are White folks who live in houses in the suburbs (maybe the
people who the narrator notices on the train).

The room was quiet as students contemplated how different characters
might view the images. When we came back together as a whole group,
they were surprised about the multiplicity of responses. June said, "I never thought about if the ladies at church would have seen Tash at a gay
parade." Jill asked her, "Do you think they would look at him differently than they look at him when he's at church?" Jonah took the question,
"Maybe, but the people at my church love everyone, so maybe not!" In
this work, students were considering how people in different communities
would think about people with specific identities, but because the specific
identities indicated race or gender performance or sexuality and were also
contextualized by a story that they were highly engaged in, students had an
explicit opportunity to consider how different layers or aspects of identities
mattered in different situations. Combining the images and the characters'
perspectives encouraged students to engage in conversations about intersectional identities.

This activity made thinking about characters' identities and their experiences more concrete and served to remind students that in this text, as in
all texts, identity and how identities intersect matter. The activity even became a touchstone to understanding other plot points and characters in the
story. When the students found out that D Foster's mama is a White woman, for example, they were shocked. Jill asked them to imagine rereading
the book with this knowledge. "Oh, like that picture thing?" one student
asked, referring to the picture walk activity and recognizing how this new
information would change the view through which he saw the story.

SPECIFIC AND INTENTIONAL ENGLISH
LANGUAGE ARTS TEACHING

While students' reading and learning around these larger themes had been
powerful, Rose was also required to teach more formal ELA writing skills.
The students in this class often made sophisticated connections in their reading and talk; however, some could not easily translate those oral discussions
to written words. They were still 5th-graders who needed the support of a
teacher to remind them not to forget commas, and that, yes, a paragraph

has at least four sentences. We know that some readers might think that these students are different from the students in their own schools for myriad reasons—it is a private school, or the class size is smaller, or it is in a different region of the United States. Of course all students are different; however, as in most classrooms, the students in this class had a range of abilities and interests, put grammar lessons to use with varying skill, and needed different levels of support to get their ideas onto the page.

As a culminating activity for this unit, Jill created a "character dive" assignment specifically to support the wide range of writing abilities of the students in the class. Students had the opportunity to pick from a list of genre options and communicate their understanding of a character through that format. As an outlining activity, students selected a genre and character they planned to focus on and wrote a rationale for their choice. One particularly skilled writer chose to write a three-act play, and another who is a gifted artist decided to create a comic strip. All the other students decided to write a series of letters. (See Figure 7.1 for the full assignment.)

Lindsay, for example, chose Tash as the character to focus on, writing letters to and from Tash and each of the main characters in the book.

Dear Tash,

I been thinking about you alot. I'm still working at KFC, and made enough money to get a basketball coach. I been working hard on my basketball, and I have been invited to some different colleges to play basketball. I want you to know that I'm not ashamed of who you are and who you want to be. I love you no matter who you are or what you do. You are still my big brother.

Love,

Jayjones

Looking between the lines of the letter, which is representative in style of Lindsay's and her classmates' writing, one can see Lindsay's deep understanding of Jayjones and his relationship to Tash. Lindsay shows her reader that she knows what is important to Jayjones (basketball), that she knows that Jayjones and others in his family have to work hard for the things that they want (his parents are not able to provide extras like a private basketball coach, but he has a job so that he can reach his goals), and that playing college basketball is important to him. Likewise, her choice of Tash as the focus of her project is reflective of the time spent discussing Tash's complex role in the family and in the overall text. Her choice to focus on Tash also provides more space for Lindsay and readers of her letter to consider LGBTQ identities and how they matter in the everyday lives of people. And, because this particular book, unlike any of the other LGBTQ-inclusive books that the class had read together, is about a Black LGBTQ character, Lindsay and her readers will consider LGBTQ identities as intersectional. Lindsay captures the class's conversations about the relationship between

Figure 7.1. *After Tupac and D Foster* "Character Dive" Assignment

In this project, you will explore one of the characters in the book to have deeper understanding not only of that character but also of the story and the context in which the story takes place. You may pick any character from the character list and any genre from the genre list. If you want to try a genre not on the list, get my permission first.

Characters to choose from:

- The Narrator
- Neeka
- D Foster
- Jayjones
- Tash
- Miss Irene

Genres to choose from:

- Letters both to and from your chosen character and all other characters on the list
- A series of diary entries by your character during and after the time that the book covers
- Comic strip (include dialogue, and a paragraph with at least 4 sentences introducing the strip)
- Research-based essay on one of the topics brought up in the book with an exploration of how that topic affects your chosen character's life
- 3-act play

No matter the genre, each project must:

- Be written legibly. If you choose a comic strip or other handwritten forms, attend to neatness.
- Include dialogue that sounds like the characters but, like Woodson, write other portions in standardized written English. Dialect can be important to bring characters to life, but it reads as disrespectful if you try to use a dialect that is not yours in other areas.
- Integrate information about at least one of these research topics and how it influenced the life of your character: foster care, hip-hop, the Black Panthers, rates of incarceration and arrest for African Americans in the 1990s, percentages of high school athletes who become professional athletes. If you want to draw on one of these topics, but haven't researched it yet, remember that your classmates who did should still have their resources, so you can ask them.
- Show the reader what is important to your character, how your character reacts to different situations and why—this might be where your research comes in!—and what you imagine your character's Big Purpose to be.
- Be turned in as a final draft appropriately edited for capital letters, punctuation, spelling, and correct homophones (like there, their, and they're).

Jayjones and Tash when she writes, "I love you no matter who you are." By working to translate their ideas into written format, students continue to develop their thinking and create products that can be shared with others, thereby extending their learning.

In this unit, representations of LGBTQ people were expanded for a class of 5th-graders. Because this was not the first book engaged with LGBTQ topics that they'd read, they had to work to interrupt the single story of LGBTQ people as White and middle-class that they had become familiar with. This expanded their prior knowledge in ways that highlighted intersectional identities. This offers students the opportunity to create deeper understandings of how power and identity are related, and to notice how combinations of identities lead to different life experiences. Comparing a White gay character like Joe in Howe's (2005) *Totally Joe* to a Black gay character like Tash can help students see not only that there are multiple ways to "be gay," but that race informs the opportunities that a gay person has access to. If students see only single-story representations of LGBTQ people, the multiplicity of experiences that are in the world could be erased for them. This reifies the invisibility of traditionally marginalized people in the LGBTQ community. Literacy practices that are present in many 5th-grade ELA classrooms, such as daily writing, extended time for thinking, read-alouds, and exploring multiple genres, enhanced the ways that students developed understanding of these complex ideas as well as ELA content related to plot, character, and theme.

STOP AND THINK

As you think about your own classroom, what pieces of this unit feel possible? How can you tie together ideas from previous chapters to ideas presented here to expand representations of LGBTQ people in your own teaching?

- What texts or media do you know of that you could combine with *After Tupac and D Foster* to expand representations of LGBTQ identities?
- What ELA standards do you see present in the read-aloud and homework activities that went along with this text? Does it help you feel more confident about including *After Tupac and D Foster* in your curriculum?
- Where are there moments or people in your own teaching that you could use to expand representations by talking explicitly about multiple identities, including LGBTQ identities?

Mapping Out Your Journey

Making a Plan and Finding Your Resources

I like the language that teachers "teach inclusively." Because first of all it helps frame it for parents in a way that is more palatable for anybody who might have an issue. . . . It has to have a real valid purpose that is academic and also community based, you know what I mean? That social learning, emotional learning, academic learning. It has to have all those pieces to it.

—Maree, reflecting on the rationale behind her
LGBTQ-inclusive teaching

The portraits of practice in the preceding chapters have shown that kids *can* engage with reading, writing, and discussing LGBTQ-inclusive themes and texts in elementary school classrooms, and even *enjoy* doing so. The three approaches we've described provide options for teachers in multiple contexts and with multiple comfort levels. But wanting to teach inclusively and knowing that kids want to and can learn in this way does not eliminate the vulnerability that can come with such teaching. There is a long history of fear when it comes to LGBTQ people and children (Epstein, 1997; Wallace & VanEvery, 2000), and remnants of these views can still be found popping up when people advocate for more inclusive learning environments (see also www.splcenter.org/fighting-hate/intelligence-report/2011/10-anti-gay-myths-debunked). Therefore, we recommend that readers know the kinds of school-, district-, and state-level policies that might apply to their decisions to take on LGBTQ-inclusive teaching. We believe that it is prudent to acknowledge any risks and constraints in order for teachers to find the most effective and appropriate ways forward. This chapter is meant to help you recognize and break down barriers you feel might inhibit your ability to teach in LGBTQ-inclusive ways. We will help you recognize constraints and locate resources that can support you. We will also guide your preparations for the kind of teaching that you want and are able to do, and direct you to supportive communities of like-minded teachers who believe in the value of LGBTQ-inclusive elementary teaching. After all, safe, inclusive schools make a demonstrable difference in the lives of LGBTQ people (Kosciw, Greytak, Diaz, &

Bartkiewicz, 2010; Kosciw et al., 2016) and can make our world a better place. It might be risky, but it's what students deserve.

KNOW YOUR SOURCES OF SUPPORT

While there is much to navigate, there are also many sources of support available to assist your work. Being familiar with available resources will help you continue your professional development related to LGBTQ topics, give you ideas for your instruction, and help you know to whom to reach out should you need additional support. The national leader on LGBTQ issues in education is GLSEN (www.glsen.org). Their mission is to create safe and affirming schools for all, regardless of sexual orientation, gender identity, or gender expression. In addition to research and policy work, GLSEN also creates instructional materials, including lesson plans; sponsors local organizing around the country; and leads national programming like Day of Silence and No Name-Calling Week, inspired by James Howe's *The Misfits* (2001). GLSEN can help you understand the policies of your local context, provide research to support the importance of creating more inclusive schools, supply professional development webinars and workshops, and connect you to supportive colleagues through their Educator Network.

The Human Rights Campaign's Welcoming Schools project (www.welcomingschools.org) is another excellent source of information and resources. Focusing primarily on early childhood and elementary grades, they have resources on LGBTQ-inclusive books and on answering challenging questions, as well as two short films showing LGBTQ-inclusive teaching and learning in action. Gender Spectrum (www.genderspectrum.org) provides a wide variety of resources to create gender-sensitive and -inclusive environments for all children and teens. Their materials can be particularly helpful when making your classroom inclusive of transgender and gender creative people's experiences.

Organizations that support LGBTQ families such as the Family Equality Council (www.familyequality.org) and COLAGE (www.colage.org) can provide suggestions on how to work with LGBTQ parents and their children. They can also connect you to other resources and direct you to any local chapters or groups in your state. And finally, other state-based or local organizations related to LGBTQ youth or LGBTQ topics in schools can also be a source of support. For example, A Queer Endeavor (aqueerendeavor.org) based in Boulder, CO, supports teachers and school communities around topics of gender and sexual diversity through community support, professional development institutes for teachers, and research. The GSA Network (gsanetwork.org), based in Oakland, CA, offers teacher training to support safe schools and helps empower students to be advocates for LGBTQ equality through leadership and activist training. Many cities also have LGBTQ community centers that can connect you to local networks of LGBTQ people and resources.

Professional organizations for literacy education can also be good sources of support for your LGBTQ-inclusive ELA teaching, especially when it comes to intellectual freedom and anticensorship efforts. The National Council of Teachers of English, for example, has an Intellectual Freedom Center (www.ncte.org/action/anti-censorship) that can help should you receive any complaints about books you read. Information available includes policy statements, rationales for reading challenged books, activities to celebrate Banned Books Week, and a system for reporting a censorship challenge (secure.ncte.org/forms/reportcensorship). The American Library Association also has an Office for Intellectual Freedom where anyone facing a book challenge can get confidential support (www.ala.org/aboutala/offices/oif). For areas represented by teachers' unions, their policies and resources may also be a source of support to tap into.

KNOW YOUR LAWS AND POLICIES

State and local laws regulating education vary widely, so it's good to know the details of those that apply to you and your classroom. Sometimes laws and policies can support LGBTQ-inclusive teaching, such as when a district has an anti-bullying policy that encourages teachers to address the use of antigay put-downs and slurs. Other times, these laws might constrain the methods of teaching that are possible. Perhaps the strictest set of legal restrictions currently in place are known as the "No Promo Homo" or "Don't Say Gay" laws. These stigmatizing laws expressly forbid discussing LGBTQ people or topics at all or allow only negative discussion. Such laws are currently on the books in seven states: Alabama, Arizona, Louisiana, Mississippi, Oklahoma, South Carolina, and Texas. If you are a teacher in one of these states, it is important to read up on the specifics of these laws and keep those restrictions in mind as you decide what ways are possible for your teaching to become more inclusive. Such details matter because, as GLSEN reports, many of these laws were written to apply specifically to sexual health education. Therefore, it's possible that ELA teaching might have more leeway in certain places, although the laws are sometimes vague and misapplied to other school contexts. While we offer some guidance here, we encourage teachers to talk with their administration and get professional legal counsel around any legal matters. More information about these laws can be found on the GLSEN website (at www.glsen.org/nopromohomo).

Unfortunately, these stigmatizing laws have real consequences for educational environments. Through their National School Climate Surveys, GLSEN has found that LGBTQ-identified students in states with such laws are more likely to hear homophobic remarks from school staff, are less likely to report incidents of harassment and assault to school staff, and are less likely to report having support from educators. Moreover, when incidents occur and educators do intervene, they do so less effectively in these states (Kosciw et al., 2010). If there's any good news regarding "No Promo Homo" states, however, it's that LGBTQ students and families in these states are hungry for teachers who see and respond to their needs. If you live or teach in one of these states, even small or subtle ways you can find to implement LGBTQ-inclusive teaching will make a difference. The methods utilized by Maree, Rose, and Barbara in Part II can be especially useful in these contexts.

While laws in some places can be a source of constraint for LGBTQ-inclusive teaching, laws and policies that support safe schools often detail protections for LGBTQ students and can be a good source of positive support for justifying teachers' inclusive pedagogical decisions. Chief among these are states' and districts' nondiscrimination and anti-bullying laws and policies, known collectively as "safe school laws" (www.glsen.org/statemaps). State anti-bullying laws or district policies prohibit bullying and harassment of students in schools. State nondiscrmination laws or district policies provide protection from discrimination to LGBTQ students in schools. At the policy level, if your district has pledged to work against bullying, LGBTQ-inclusive teaching that explores how we treat people different from ourselves would fit squarely within that goal. Similarly, laws at the state level can be a source of justification for teachers who address LGBTQ topics in the classroom as a way to serve all students' needs. If, for example, a state has a nondiscrimination law protecting people on the basis of sexual orientation and gender identity, then teachers might use that information to support their decisions to use LGBTQ-inclusive texts, since censoring those texts could be considered discriminatory.

Currently, 13 states and the District of Columbia have nondiscrimination laws that apply to schools and protect students on the specific basis of sexual orientation and gender identity. Those states are California, Colorado, Connecticut, Illinois, Iowa, Maine, Massachusetts, Minnesota, New Jersey, New York, Oregon, Vermont, and Washington. Wisconsin also provides protection to students on the basis of sexual orientation, although not gender identity.

According to Kull, Kosciw, & Greytak (2015), the most effective anti-bullying and harassment laws and policies enumerate, or list, characteristics that are most frequently the subject of bullying and harassment, such as race, national origin, sexual orientation, gender identity or expression, disability, and religion. Fully enumerated anti-bullying laws that specifically prohibit bullying and harassment of students based on sexual orientation and gender identity can be important for giving teachers, students, and families something clear, specific, and concrete to point to when challenging harassing behavior or advocating for inclusive treatment in schools. For example, students in schools with enumerated policies reported that teachers intervened more often compared to students in schools both with generic anti-bullying policies and those with no anti-bullying policy at all (Kull et al., 2015). States that have enumerated anti-bullying laws that specifically protect students on the basis of both sexual orientation and gender identity include Arkansas, California, Colorado, Connecticut, Illinois, Iowa, Maine, Maryland, Massachusetts, Minnesota, Nevada, New Jersey, New York, North Carolina, Oregon, Rhode Island, Vermont, and Washington. Unfortunately, Missouri and South Dakota currently prohibit school districts from having enumerated policies, thereby weakening legal protections for LGBTQ people.

On the other hand, a few state-level laws actually *require* teaching LGBTQ information in schools. For example, California's FAIR Education Act specified that LGBTQ-inclusive history and social sciences be taught in public schools, including some lessons at the elementary school level. The California Healthy Youth Act requires all California public schools to teach about gender expression and gender stereotypes. State-specific snapshots of LGBTQ-related laws that impact education can be found on the GLSEN website (at www.glsen.org/statesnapshots).

To assure you have accurate, up-to-date information on these laws, consult directly with organizations like GLSEN (www.glsen.org), HRC (www.hrc.org/state-maps), the ACLU (www.aclu.org), or a state-level LGBTQ advocacy group (www.welcomingresources.org/stateorglinks.htm and www.equalityfederation.org/members/).

MAKING AND SUPPORTING YOUR DECISIONS

We hope reading about the three methods of LGBTQ-inclusive teaching outlined in this book and seeing snapshots of teachers putting them into practice has brought you closer to picking new texts and techniques to add to your own teaching. Before you go off to change the world, however, we want to encourage you to not just make choices about what you think will work best in your context, but also to build a rationale around those decisions. In our experience, thinking through what you want to teach and why ahead of time can help you be prepared to communicate that information in a clear and timely manner to administrators and parents who might question your decisions. While we don't think that there need be anything inherently "controversial" about LGBTQ-inclusive teaching, we know that not everyone shares that perspective. The teachers we've worked with have almost always done some type of sharing—whether at a curriculum night or parent–teacher conferences or in a welcome letter or just one-on-one with their principal—about the teaching they'll be doing, even if it's been fairly general, and they've frequently found themselves glad at later points in the

year that they'd had these initial communications. Therefore, we encourage
you to reflect on whether or not you feel it appropriate to notify people
such as parents and administrators of your plans and, if so, what you will
tell them.

Talking with Parents and Administrators

There are many ways to talk about LGBTQ-inclusive teaching, so you'll
need to think through how you're going to discuss your pedagogical
choices. For example, will you describe these efforts in a general way, such
as "teaching inclusively" or "being sure all students see themselves reflected
in the curriculum"? Or do you want to be more direct and say that you're
"teaching with LGBTQ-inclusive texts," "queering the curriculum," or
"teaching students to question the heterosexual matrix"? Clearly, these will
be personal, highly contextualized decisions. We don't know your specific
situation, so we can't tell you the "right" answer, but we can share examples to help you think through your options.

   One option is to contextualize these efforts in a larger inquiry, much like
Maree did with "Being a Problem Solver" or like Rose did with "Studying
Social Justice." You might communicate to parents and administrators at
the beginning of the year what this larger frame that guides your choices
will be and why you chose it. You could then further specify the kinds of
topics such a unit might address, perhaps even specifying that some of those
choices might involve LGBTQ inclusion, among other topics. Another option is to emphasize a value of your classroom or your school community,
perhaps by saying something like, "In Room 16, we will practice sharing
our views and listening to others." Then you might zero in and explain
some of the ways this value will show up in the context of your ELA curriculum. You might say that you'll be reading books about a wide range of
diverse people or that you want to be sure all students and their families feel
welcome in your classroom or that you're committed to responding directly
to issues of bullying you hear or that you'll encourage students to be proud
of who they are while also learning about the lives of others.

   Another recommendation for any rationale you adopt for inclusive
teaching is to focus on student learning. Being able to tie decisions around
LGBTQ-inclusive teaching to curricular expectations can help support and
justify the work. We've shown you specific ELA skills and standards like
inferences, character traits, and the use of textual evidence that you could
meet through LGBTQ-inclusive teaching. But in addition to meeting stated curricular goals, the critical thinking and perspective-taking that books
and discussions about diverse people and situations require are the kinds of
21st-century skills we want to encourage in students. We hope the examples
throughout this book have also helped you see those broader links. For example, does your district or do your standards expect you to build students'

critical thinking skills? Read and write from multiple perspectives and in multiple genres? Create safe, respectful school environments for all students? LGBTQ-inclusive teaching can be a part of that. After all, LGBTQ-inclusive teaching requires students to talk across areas of difference and notice multiple and intersecting identities, and draws attention to the often unnoticed social categories that shape our everyday lives. Connecting these "big ideas" to your school and district mission statements or learning targets are important ways to show that the goals of this work are no different from what others are trying to accomplish. Similarly, as facts about the impact of inclusive school curriculum from GLSEN (Kosciw et al., 2016) illustrate, this isn't about any kind of agenda other than safety, respect, and equitable student outcomes. This is meaningful learning.

What If Parents Aren't Supportive?

When we talk to pre- and inservice teachers about LGBTQ inclusion, the first question we inevitably get is, "But what about the parents?" Our initial response is a reminder that "parents" is not a monolithic category. Many parents actually welcome and want LGBTQ-inclusive teaching for their children. After all, Jill is the parent of school-age children and often reminds her education students that she has the ability to be just as loud and persistent in *support* of LGBTQ-inclusive teaching that honors her family as resistant parents might be against it. "Whose resistance are you more worried about?" It's not a question she expects them to answer, but it is one she expects them to think about.

Drawing on our experiences and those of the teachers with whom we work, we know that anticipating parental resistance about any of our teaching choices can be nerve-racking. In the end, however, such anticipation can actually help alleviate some of that resistance by encouraging teachers to be careful and thoughtful about their choices. For example, written communications with your students' families at the beginning of the school year about your values, visions, and goals creates documentation you can return to should a parent later feel that they weren't informed of your plan to teach inclusively. Often, listening to and understanding a family's concerns for their child can go a long way.

This is a technique Maree and Rose have both used when parents challenged their read-aloud choices, including *Totally Joe* and *George*. Rose, for example, had a blog that she updated weekly that informed parents about read-alouds and ongoing projects. Likewise, at the beginning of the school year, she informed parents both in writing and at Open House that the class would be studying issues of equity. Later in the year, when a parent was concerned about how the class was focusing on gender, Rose was able to point to that communication and to connect the class's learning to broader concepts of social justice and understanding differences. By listening to the parent rather than getting defensive, and recognizing where the misunderstanding was situated, both Rose and the parent left the meeting feeling heard and with a deeper understanding of the curriculum. When dealt with in this way, parents can know their concerns have been heard. Talking with parents about the reasons why your choices are appropriate for your class and curriculum positions you as an expert who is open and willing to share your professional knowledge with anyone—parent or other—who asks. Show evidence (maybe even this book!) that children at these ages *can* handle discussions of LGBTQ topics, and remind parents of the mission of the class, the school, and the district. When family members of Maree's students saw the depth of conversations the students were able to have around LGBTQ topics, they often felt more comfortable with inclusive teaching. Openness often invites discussion with the families of students, and it is during these discussions that teachers can explain how the book or unit at issue helps to teach the required curricular standards.

Finally, remember that families should always be allowed to make decisions or modify activities *for their own children.* That is completely within their rights, and those decisions deserve your cooperation. What parents do not have the right to do, however, is alter the curriculum for the rest of the class. If a family is not comfortable with a particular book, their children should not have to read it, but they should not keep other students from reading it either. When working with a family to adjust instruction for an individual student, teachers may want to consult with their administration about how to put such a plan into practice. One possible solution could be the parents asking their child to avoid certain books during independent reading. To modify whole-class instruction, perhaps the student reads alternative texts in another room while you and the class read the LGBTQ-inclusive text, or the child completes a parallel assignment that covers the same skills, but with different content than what the other students in class are working on. These are things that Maree and Rose have done successfully that are always options for your own situation. Maree, for example, worked with parents who objected to their daughter reading *Totally Joe.* Together, they agreed that their daughter would not participate in the reading or discussion of the book and decided on alternative work that the child would do in another room.

CLOSING THOUGHTS

Schools are complicated places where people and ideas and cultures and communities all come together. They are dynamic, messy, exciting microcosms of our larger world. Schools and the adults in them help to shape how students envision themselves, who they can be, and how they might be seen outside of the walls of their formal education. As teachers, we have the great responsibility of providing examples for our children of the world around them—people who are both like us and who are not, all of whom deserve to be recognized for our full humanity. When ELA teachers expand their curriculum to make room for LGBTQ people and communities, they open windows and shine light on mirrors for all of their students.

STOP AND THINK

As you reflect on how Maree, Rose, Barbara, and other teachers put theories about LGBTQ-inclusive teaching into practice, consider your own context, the LGBTQ-inclusive teaching you want to do, and the LGBTQ-inclusive teaching you might already be engaged in. Our hope is that with trial and error, practice, and collaboration with other teachers, you find a rhythm with LGBTQ-inclusive ELA teaching that is meaningful and sustainable. To that end, we're asking you to Stop and Think one last time in this book and consider what tools you can take with you.

- Are there curricular ideas from Parts I, II, and III that you can do next week? Next month? Next year?
- What ELA practices that you already use easily map onto the examples from teachers in Parts I, II, and III? How can you make these practices (more) LGBTQ-inclusive?
- What books or materials do you already have that you can use? What new books or additional materials will you need?
- What feels difficult or even scary about these three approaches? How can you challenge yourself and your students to overcome those sticky places?
- What are your short-term and long-term goals for this work that you'll use to guide your choices?

Appendix

It might help teachers get started with LGBTQ-inclusive teaching if they have an easily accessible place to find resources. Here, we've included book-lists and media links that teachers can use to find classroom materials, as well as a list of websites and links for lesson plans using LGBTQ-inclusive books and themes. Finally, we've included links to glossaries of words related to LGBTQ identities, gender, and sexuality.

CLASSROOM MATERIALS

We are heartened to find that every year there are more titles with LGBTQ characters and themes for elementary-school-age readers. As the culture shifts toward more welcoming attitudes about the LGBTQ community, these texts have relied less and less on stereotypes. We want to caution read-ers to make sure that the books they choose to share with their students are high quality and avoid stereotyping traditionally marginalized identities. The same criteria that guide selections of other multicultural books apply here. These are some things to look for: (1) The authors of the texts are members of the LGBTQ community, or are allies who have been working in the community for a long time; (2) the book is historically accurate; and (3) the book does not set people from different traditionally marginalized groups against each other.

While every book can be critiqued in some way, below is a list of some of our go-to LGBTQ-inclusive books that fit these basic criteria and that can serve as a good starting point for teachers to use in the kinds of teaching we've outlined in this book, many of which you've already heard about in the preceding chapters. We hope that teachers are able to continue adding to these lists as more and more books are published.

Suggested Picture Book Titles

10,000 Dresses by Marcus Ewert
And Tango Makes Three by Justin Richardson and Peter Parnell
Antonio's Card / La Tarjeta de Antonio by Rigoberto González

Call Me Tree / Llamame Arbol by Maya Christina Gonzalez
The Different Dragon by Jennifer Bryan
Donovan's Big Day by Leslea Newman
The Family Book by Todd Parr
The Harvey Milk Story by Kari Krakow
I Am Jazz by Jessica Herthel
In Our Mothers' House by Patricia Polacco
It's OK to Be Different by Todd Parr
Jacob's New Dress by Sarah Hoffman and Ian Hoffman
King and King by Linda de Haan
Large Fears by Myles E. Johnson
Morris Micklewhite and the Tangerine Dress by Christine
    Baldacchino
My Princess Boy by Cheryl Kilodavis
Not Every Princess by Jeffrey Bone and Lisa Bone
Oliver Button Is a Sissy by Tomie dePaola
Pride: The Story of Harvey Milk and the Rainbow Flag by Rob
    Sanders
Red: A Crayon's Story by Michael Hall
The Sissy Duckling by Harvey Fierstein
A Tale of Two Daddies by Vanita Oelschlager
A Tale of Two Mommies by Vanita Oelschlager
This Day in June by Gayle E. Pitman
*When You Look Out the Window: How Phyllis Lyon and Del Martin
    Built a Community* by Gayle E. Pitman
William's Doll by Charlotte Zolotow

List other titles you've used or found here:

_____

_____

_____

Suggested Chapter Book Titles

After Tupac and D Foster by Jacqueline Woodson
Better Nate Than Ever by Tim Federle
George by Alex Gino
The Misfits by James Howe
The Popularity Papers series by Amy Ignatow
Totally Joe by James Howe
The War That Saved My Life by Kimberly Brubaker Bradley

List other titles you've used or found here:

_____

_____

_____

Suggested Media Resources

Creating Gender Inclusive Schools—video by Jonathan Skurnik
  and Gender Spectrum. Available from Gender Spectrum at www.
  genderspectrum.org/creating-gender-inclusive-schools/
It's Elementary: Talking About Gay Issues in Schools—video and
  curriculum. Available from Groundspark Media at groundspark.
  org/our-films-and-campaigns/elementary
That's A Family—video and curriculum. Available from Groundspark
  Media at groundspark.org/our-films-and-campaigns/thatfamily
*Tomboy: A Short Film About Gender Exploration for Young
  Children*—video by Barb Taylor. Available from Vimeo at vimeo.
  com/10772672
What Can We Do? Bias, Bullying & Bystanders—video and
  curriculum. Available from HRC's Welcoming Schools at www.
  welcomingschools.org/our-films/what-can-we-do/
What Do You Know? Kids Talk About LGBTQ Topics—video and
  curriculum. Available from HRC's Welcoming Schools at www.
  welcomingschools.org/our-films/what-do-you-know/

List other media resources you've used or found here:

_____

_____

_____

LESSON PLANNING MATERIALS

Educators across the country are creating and sharing LGBTQ-inclusive
lesson plans. Here are some sites with examples that might serve as good
starting points for your work.

And Tango Makes Three Lesson Plans: Grades K–5. Available from
  Support Services for LGBTQ Youth, San Francisco Unified School

District, at www.healthiersf.org/LGBTQ/InTheClassroom/docs/
curriculum/Tango%20Makes%203_revised2.pdf

King and King Lesson Plans: Grades 3–5. Available from Support
Services for LGBTQ Youth, San Francisco Unified School District,
at www.healthiersf.org/LGBTQ/InTheClassroom/docs/curriculum/
King%20%20King.pdf

Lesson Plans to Make LGBTQ-Inclusive Elementary Schools.
Available from HRC's Welcoming Schools at www.
welcomingschools.org/resources/lesson-plans/lgbtq-inclusive-
schools/lgbtq-with-books/

LGBTQ-Inclusive Lesson Plans for Elementary Classrooms. Available
from A Queer Endeavor at aqueerendeavor.org/for-educators/

Ready, Set, Respect! Elementary Toolkit. Available from GLSEN at
www.glsen.org/readysetrespect

LINKS TO LGBTQ GLOSSARIES

This list of links can help readers remain up to date with terms and definitions used by and for the LGBTQ community.

Glossary of Terms. Human Rights Campaign. Available at www.hrc.
org/resources/glossary-of-terms

Glossary. The Trevor Project's Trevor Support Center. Available at
www.thetrevorproject.org/trvr_support_center/glossary/

National Glossary of Terms. PFLAG. Available at www.pflag.org/
glossary

Children's Literature Cited

Abramchik, L. (1993). *Is your family like mine?* (A. Bradshaw, Illus.). Brooklyn, NY: Open Heart, Open Mind.

Andreae, G. (2001). *Giraffes can't dance.* (G. Parker-Rees, Illus.). New York, NY: Scholastic.

Buchanan, A. J., & Peskowitz, M. (2009). *The daring book for girls.* New York, NY: HarperCollins.

Carr, J. (2010). *Be who you are!* (B. Rumback, Illus.). Bloomington, IN: Author House.

de Haan, L., & Nijland, S. (2002). *King and king.* Berkeley, CA: Tricycle Press.

dePaola, T. (1979). *Oliver Button is a sissy.* New York, NY: Simon & Schuster.

DiCamillo, K. (2003). *The tale of Despereaux.* Cambridge, MA: Candlewick Press.

DiCamillo, K. (2009). *Because of Winn Dixie.* Cambridge, MA: Candlewick Press.

Ewert, M. (2008). *10,000 dresses.* (R. Ray, Illus.). New York, NY: Triangle Square.

Gino, A. (2015). *George.* New York, NY: Scholastic.

Hall, M. (2015). *Red: A crayon's story.* New York, NY: HarperCollins.

Henkes, K. (1988). *Chester's way.* New York, NY: Mulberry Paperbacks.

Howe, J. (2001). *The misfits.* New York, NY: Atheneum Books for Young Readers.

Howe, J. (2005).*Totally Joe.* New York, NY: Atheneum Books for Young Readers.

Iggulden, C., & Iggulden, H. (2007). *The dangerous book for boys.* New York, NY: HarperCollins.

Kelly, J. (2009). *The evolution of Calpurnia Tate.* New York, NY: Square Fish.

Kilodavis, C. (2009). *My princess boy.* (S. DeSimone, Illus.). Seattle, WA: KD Talent.

Lowry, L. (1989). *Number the stars.* New York, NY: HMH Books for Young Readers.

Lowry, L. (1993). *The giver.* New York, NY: Dell Laurel-Leaf.

McKissack, P. (2007). *A friendship for today.* New York, NY: Scholastic.

Newman, L. 2011). *Donovan's big day.* (M. Dutton, Illus.). Berkeley, CA: Tricycle Press.

Patterson, K. (1977). *Bridge to Terabithia.* New York, NY: HarperCollins.

Pearsall, S. (2005). *Crooked river.* New York, NY: Yearling.

Polacco, P. (2009). *In our mothers' house.* New York, NY: Philomel.

Richardson, J., & Parnell, P. (2005). *And Tango makes three.* (H. Cole, Illus.). New York, NY: Simon & Schuster.

Ryan, P. M. (2000). *Esperanza rising.* New York, NY: Scholastic.

Sendak, M. (1963). *Where the wild things are.* New York, NY: Harper & Row.

Skutch, R. (1995). *Who's in a family?* (L. Nienhaus, Illus.). Berkeley, CA: Tricycle Press.

Spinelli, J. (1990). *Maniac Magee.* Boston, MA: Little, Brown.

Taylor, M. (1987). *The friendship.* New York, NY: Dial.

Willhoite, M. (1990). *Daddy's roommate.* Boston, MA: Alyson Wonderland.

Woodson, J. (2001). *The other side* (E. B. Lewis, Illus.). New York, NY: Putnam.

Woodson, J. (2008). *After Tupac and D Foster.* New York, NY: Puffin Books.

Woodson, J. (2012). *Each kindness* (E. B. Lewis, Illus.). New York, NY: Nancy Paulsen.

References

Adams, R., & Persinger, J. (2013). School support and same-sex parents. *Communique, 42*(2), 1, 10–13.

Adichie, C. N. (2009, July). *The danger of a single story* [Video file]. Retrieved from www.ted.com/talks/chimamanda_adichie_the_danger_of_a_single_story

American Academy of Pediatrics (2015). *Gender non-conforming and transgender children*. Retrieved from www.healthychildren.org/English/ages-stages/grade-school/Pages/Gender-Non-Conforming-Transgender-Children.aspx

Athanases, S. (1996). A gay-themed lesson in an ethnic literature curriculum: Tenth graders' responses to "Dear Anita." *Harvard Educational Review 66*(2), 231–257.

Bell, J. (Executive Producer). (2011, January 3). *The Today Show* [Television broadcast]. New York, NY: National Broadcasting Company.

Bishop, R. S. (1990). Mirrors, windows, and sliding glass doors. *Perspective, 6*(3), ix–xi.

Blackburn, M. V. (2002). Disrupting the (hetero)normative: Exploring literacy performances and identity work with queer youth. *Journal of Adolescent & Adult Literacy, 46*(4), 312–324.

Blackburn, M. V. (2003). Exploring literacy performances and power dynamics at The Loft: Queer youth reading the world and the word. *Research in the Teaching of English, 37*(4), 467–490.

Blackburn, M. V. (2005). Disrupting dichotomies for social change: A review of, critique of, and complement to current educational literacy scholarship on gender. *Research in the Teaching of English, 39*(4), 398–416.

Blackburn, M. V., & Buckley, J. F. (2005). Teaching queer-inclusive English language arts. *Journal of Adolescent & Adult Literacy, 49*(3), 202–212.

Blackburn, M. V., Clark, C. T., Kenney, L. M., & Smith, J. M. (2010). *Acting out! Combating homophobia through teacher activism*. New York, NY: Teachers College Press.

Blaise, M. (2005). *Playing it straight: Uncovering gender discourses in the early childhood classroom*. New York, NY: Routledge.

Brill, S. A., & Pepper, R. (2008*). The transgender child: A handbook for families and professionals*. Berkeley, CA: Cleis Press.

Britton, J. (1970). *Language and learning*. Coral Gables, FL: University of Miami Press.

Britzman, D. (1995). Is there a queer pedagogy? Or, stop reading straight. *Educational Theory, 45*(2), 151–165.

Butler, J. (1999). *Gender trouble* (2nd ed.). New York, NY: Routledge.

Butler, S. (Director and Producer). (2012). *Cracking the codes: The system of racial inequality* [DVD]. Oakland, CA: World Trust Educational Services.

Casper, V., & Schultz, S. (1999). *Gay parents/straight schools: Building communication and trust.* New York, NY: Teachers College Press.

Clark, C. T., & Blackburn, M. V. (2009). Reading LGBT-themed literature with young people: What's possible? *English Journal, 98*(4), 28–32.

Cohen, C. (1997). Punks, bulldaggers, and welfare queens. *GLQ: A Journal of Lesbian and Gay Studies, 3,* 437–465.

Cowhey, M. (2006). *Black ants and Buddhists: Thinking critically and teaching differently in the primary grades.* Portland, ME: Stenhouse.

Crenshaw, K. (1991). Mapping the margins: Intersectionality, identity politics, and violence against women of color. In K. Crenshaw, N. Gotanda, G. Peller, & K. Thomas (Eds.), *Critical race theory: Key writings that formed the movement* (pp. 357–383). New York, NY: The New Press.

Daniels, H. (2002). *Literature circles: Voice and choice in book clubs and reading groups.* Portland, ME: Stenhouse.

DePalma, R., & Atkinson, E. (2006). The sound of silence: Talking about sexual orientation and schooling. *Sex Education, 6*(4), 333–349.

DePalma, R., & Atkinson, E. (2009). *Interrogating heteronormativity in primary schools: The work of the No Outsiders Project.* London, UK: Trentham.

Dozier, C., Johnston, P., & Rogers, R. (2006). *Critical literacy/critical teaching: Tools for preparing responsive teachers.* New York, NY: Teachers College Press.

Dutro, E. (2001). "But that's a girls' book!" Exploring gender boundaries in children's reading practices. *The Reading Teacher, 55*(4), 376–384.

Dutro, E. (2009). Children writing "hard times": Lived experiences of poverty and the class-privileged assumptions of a mandated curriculum. *Language Arts, 87*(2), 89–98.

Dutro, E., Kazemi, E., & Balf, R. (2006). Making sense of "The Boy Who Died": Tales of a struggling successful writer. *Reading and Writing Quarterly, (22)*4, 325–356.

Dyson, A. H., & Genishi, C. (Eds.). (1994). *The need for story: Cultural diversity in classroom and community.* Urbana, IL: National Council of Teachers of English.

Emdin, C. (2016). *For White folks who teach in the hood and the rest of y'all, too: Reality pedagogy and urban education.* New York, NY: Beacon Press.

Enciso, P. (2004). Reading discrimination. In S. Greene & D. Abt-Perkins (Eds.), *Making race visible: Literacy research for cultural understanding* (pp. 149–177). New York, NY: Teachers College.

Epstein, D. (1997). Cultures of schooling/cultures of sexuality. *International Journal of Inclusive Education, 1*(1), 37–53.

Epstein, D. (2000). Reading gender, reading sexualities: Children and the negotiation of meaning in "alternative" texts. In W. Spurlin (Ed.), *Lesbian and gay studies and the teaching of English* (pp. 213–233). Urbana, IL: National Council of Teachers of English.

Foucault, M. (1977/1995). *Discipline and punish*. New York, NY: Vintage.

Freire, P. (1994). *Pedagogy of the oppressed*. New York, NY: Continuum. (Original work published 1970)

Freire, P., & Macedo, D. (1987). *Literacy: Reading the word and the world*. South Hadley, MA: Bergen & Garvey.

Gadsden, V. (1993). Literacy, education, and identity among African-Americans: The communal nature of learning. *Urban Education, 27*(4), 352–369.

Gates, G. J. (2014). *LGB families and relationships: Analyses of the 2013 National Health Interview Survey*. Los Angeles, CA: Williams Institute, UCLA School of Law.

Gates, G. J. (2015). *Comparing LGBTQ rankings by metro area: 1990 to 2014*. Los Angeles, CA: Williams Institute, UCLA School of Law.

Gates, G. J. (2017, January 11). In US, more adults identifying as LGBT. *Gallup News*. Retreived from news.gallup.com/poll/201731/lgbt-identification-rises .aspx

Gatto, L. (2013). "Lunch is gross": Gaining access to powerful literacies. *Language Arts, 90*(4), 241–252.

GLSEN & Harris Interactive. (2012). *Playgrounds and prejudice: Elementary school climate in the United States, A survey of students and teachers*. New York, NY: GLSEN.

Harris, V. (1992). Multiethnic children's literature. In K. D. Wood & A. Moss (Eds.), *Exploring literature in the classroom: Content and methods* (pp. 169–201). Norwood, MA: Christopher Gordon.

Harste, J. C. (2014). Transmediation: What art affords our understanding of literacy. In P. Dunston, S. Fullerton, M. Cole, D. Herro, J. Malloy, P. Wilder, and K. Headley (Eds.), *63rd yearbook of the Literacy Research Association* (pp. 88–103). Altamonte Springs, FL: Literacy Research Association.

Hermann-Wilmarth, J. M. (2007). Full inclusion: Understanding the role of gay and lesbian texts and films in teacher education classrooms. *Language Arts, 84*(4), 347–356.

Hermann-Wilmarth, J. M. (2008). Creating dialogic spaces among preservice teachers and teacher educators. *Teachers College Record*. Retrieved from www .tcrecord.org (ID Number: 15189)

Hermann-Wilmarth, J. M. (2010). More than book talks: Preservice teacher dialogue after reading gay and lesbian children's literature. *Language Arts, 87*(3), 188–198.

Hermann-Wilmarth, J. M., Lannen, R., & Ryan, C. L. (2017). Critical literacy and transgender topics in an upper elementary classroom: A portrait of possibility. *Journal of Language & Literacy Education, 13*(1), 15–27.

Hermann-Wilmarth, J. M., & Ryan, C. L. (2015a). Doing what you can: Considering ways to address LGBT topics in language arts curricula. *Language Arts*, *92*(6), 436–443.

Hermann-Wilmarth, J. M., & Ryan, C. L. (2015b). Destabilizing the homonormative for young readers: Exploring Tash's queerness in Jacqueline Woodson's *After Tupac and D Foster*. In D. Linville & D. Carlson (Eds.), *Beyond borders: Queer eros and ethos (ethics) in LGBTQ young adult literature* (pp. 85–99). New York, NY: Peter Lang.

Hermann-Wilmarth, J. M., & Ryan, C. L. (2016). Queering chapter books with LGBT characters for young readers: Recognizing and complicating representations of homonormativity. *Discourse: Studies in the Cultural Politics of Education, 37*(6), 846–866.

Hermann-Wilmarth, J. M., & Souto-Manning, M. (2007). Queering early childhood practices: Opening up possibilities with common children's literature. *International Journal for Equity and Innovation in Early Childhood, 5*(2), 5–16.

Janks, H. (2000). Domination, access, diversity, and design: A synthesis for critical literacy education. *Educational Review, 52*(2), 15–30.

Jenkins, H. (2006). *Confronting the challenges of participatory culture: Media education for the 21st century* (White paper). Chicago, IL: Macarthur Foundation. Accessed online at www.macfound.org/media/article_pdfs/JENKINS_WHITE _PAPER.PDF

Jones, S. (2006). *Girls, social class, and literacy: What teachers can do to make a difference*. Portsmouth, NH: Heinemann.

Jones, S. (2012). Critical literacies in the making: Social class and identities in the early reading classroom. *Journal of Early Childhood Literacies, 13*(2), 197–224.

Jones, S., Clarke, L., & Enriquez, G. (2010). *The reading turn-around: A five-part framework for differentiated instruction (grades 2–5)*. New York, NY: Teachers College Press.

Kehily, M. J. (2004). Boys and girls: Sexuality as performance in the primary school. *Education 3–13: International Journal of Primary, Elementary, and Early Years Education, 32*(2), 65–72.

Kidd, K. (1998). Introduction: Lesbian/gay literature for children and young adults. *Children's Literature Association Quarterly, 23*(3), 114–119.

Kosciw, J. G., Greytak, E. A., Bartkiewicz, M. J., Boesen, M. J., & Palmer, N. A. (2012). *The 2011 National School Climate Survey: The experiences of lesbian, gay, bisexual and transgender youth in our nation's schools*. New York, NY: GLSEN.

Kosciw, J. G., Greytak, E. A., Diaz, E. M., & Bartkiewicz, M. J. (2010). *The 2009 National School Climate Survey: The experiences of lesbian, gay, bisexual and transgender youth in our nation's schools*. New York, NY: GLSEN.

Kosciw, J. G., Greytak, E. A., Giga, N. M., Villenas, C., & Danischewski, D. J. (2016). *The 2015 National School Climate Survey: The experiences of lesbian, gay, bisexual, transgender, and queer youth in our nation's schools, Executive summary*. New York, NY: GLSEN.

Kull, R. M., Kosciw, J. G., & Greytak, E. A. (2015). *From statehouse to school-house: Anti-bullying policy efforts in U.S. states and school districts.* New York, NY: GLSEN.

Kumashiro, K. (2002). *Troubling education: Queer activism and antioppressive ped-agogy.* New York, NY: Routledge.

Ladson-Billings, G. (1995). Toward a theory of culturally relevant pedagogy. *American Educational Research Journal, 32*(3), 465–491.

Leibowitz, S. F., & Spack, N. P. (2011). The development of a gender identity psy-chosocial clinic: Treatment issues, logistical considerations, interdisciplinary cooperation, and future initiatives. *Child and Adolescent Psychiatric Clinics of North America, 20*, 701–724.

Lester, J. Z. (2014). Homonormativity in children's literature: An intersectional anal-ysis of queer-themed picture books. *Journal of LGBT Youth, 11*(3), 244–275.

Letts, W., & Sears, J. (Eds.). (1999). *Queering elementary education: Advancing the dialogue about sexualities and schooling.* Lanham, MD: Rowman & Littlefield.

Lewison, M., Flint, A. S., & Van Sluys, K. (2002). Taking on critical literacy: The journey of newcomers and novices. *Language Arts, 79*(5), 382–392.

Lorde, A. (1984). *Sister outsider: Essays and speeches.* Freedom, CA: The Crossing Press.

Meier, C., & Harris, J. (n.d.). Fact sheet: Gender diversity and transgender identi-ty in children. Washington, DC: Society for the Psychological Study of LGBT Issues, American Psychological Association Division 44. Retrieved from www .apadivisions.org/division-44/resources/advocacy/transgender-children.pdf

Meyer, E., Tilland-Stafford, A., & Airton, L. (2016). Transgender and gender cre-ative students in PK–12 schools: What we can learn from their teachers. *Teach-ers College Record, 118*(8), 1–50.

Moje, E., Luke, A., Davies, B., & Street, B. (2009). Literacy and identity: Examining the metaphors in history and contemporary research. *Reading Research Quar-terly, 44*(4), 415–437.

Morrell, E. (2007). *Critical literacy and urban youth: Pedagogies of access, dissent, and liberation.* New York, NY: Routledge.

Olson, K. R., Durwood, L., DeMeules, M., & McLaughlin, K. A. (2016). Mental health of transgender children who are supported in their identities. *Pediatrics, 137*(3), 1–8.

Payne, E., & Smith, M. J. (2012). Safety, celebration and risk: Educator responses to LGBTQ professional development. *Teaching Education, 23*(3), 265–285.

Pinar, W. (Ed.). (1998). *Queer theory in education.* Mahwah, NJ: Lawrence Erlbaum.

Quinlivan, K., & Town, S. (1999). Queer pedagogy, educational practice and lesbian and gay youth. *Qualitative Studies in Education, 12*(5), 509–524.

Renold, E. (2005). *Girls, boys, and junior sexualities: Exploring children's gen-der and sexual relations in the primary school.* Abingdon, United Kingdom: Routledge.

Rich, A. (1980). Compulsory heterosexuality and lesbian existence. *Signs: Journal of Women in Culture and Society, 5*(4), 631–660.

Robinson, K. H. (2005). "Queerying" gender: Heteronormativity in early childhood education. *Australian Journal of Early Childhood, 30*(2), 19–28.

Rosenblatt, L. (1938). *Literature as exploration* (5th ed.). New York, NY: Modern Language Association of America.

Rosenblatt, L. (1956). The acid test for literature teaching. *English Journal, 45*(2), 66–74.

Ryan, C. L. (2010a). *"How do you spell family?": Literacy, heteronormativity, and young children of lesbian mothers* (Doctoral dissertation, Ohio State University). Available from ProQuest Dissertations and Theses database. (UMI No. 3425382)

Ryan, C. L. (2010b). Talking, reading and writing lesbian and gay families in classrooms: The consequences of different pedagogical approaches. In C. Compton-Lilly & S. Greene (Eds.), *Bedtime stories and book reports: Connecting parent involvement and family literacy* (pp. 96–108). New York, NY: Teachers College Press.

Ryan, C. L. (2016). Kissing brides and loving hot vampires: Children's construction and perpetuation of heteronormativity in elementary school classrooms. *Sex Education, 16*(1), 77–90.

Ryan, C. L., & Hermann-Wilmarth, J. M. (2013). Already on the shelf: Queer readings of award-winning children's literature. *Journal of Literacy Research, 45*(2), 142–172.

Ryan, C. L., Patraw, J., & Bednar, M. (2013). Discussing princess boys and pregnant men: Teaching about gender diversity and transgender experiences within an elementary school curriculum. *Journal of LGBT Youth 10*(1–2), 83–105.

Schall, J., & Kauffmann, G. (2003). Exploring literature with gay and lesbian characters in the elementary school. *Journal of Children's Literature, 29*(1), 36–45.

Siegel, M. (1995). More than words: The generative power of transmediation for learning. *Canadian Journal of Education, 20*(4), 455–475.

Sipe, L. (2002). Talking back and taking over: Young children's expressive engagement during storybook read-alouds. *The Reading Teacher, 55*(5), 476–483.

Souto-Manning, M. (2013). *Multicultural teaching in the early childhood classroom.* New York, NY: Teachers College Press

Souto-Manning, M., & Hermann-Wilmarth, J. M. (2008). Teacher inquiries into gay and lesbian families in early childhood classrooms. *Journal of Early Childhood Research, 6*(3), 263–280.

Staley, S., & Leonardi, B. (2016). Leaning in to discomfort: Preparing literacy teachers for gender and sexual diversity. *Research in the Teaching of English, 51*(2), 209–229.

Substance Abuse and Mental Health Services Administration. (2014). *A practitioner's resource guide: Helping families to support their LGBT children* (HHS Publication No. PEP14-LGBTKIDS). Rockville, MD: Substance Abuse and Mental Health Services Administration.

Sumara, D., & Davis, B. (1998). Telling tales of surprise. In W. Pinar (Ed.), *Queer theory in education* (pp. 197–219). Mahwah, NJ: Lawrence Erlbaum.

Tschida, C. M., Ryan, C. L., & Ticknor, A. S. (2014). Building on windows and mirrors: Encouraging the disruption of "single stories" through children's literature. *Journal of Children's Literature, 40*(1), 28–39. Retrieved at www .childrensliteratureassembly.org/docs/JCL-40-1-Article_Tschida.pdf

Tyson, C. (1999). "Shut my mouth wide open": Realistic fiction and social action. *Theory Into Practice, 38*(3), 155–159.

Vasquez, V. (2004). *Negotiating critical literacies with young children.* Mahwah, NJ: Lawrence Erlbaum.

Wallace, A., & VanEvery, J. (2000). Sexuality in the primary school. *Sexualities, 3*(4), 409–423.

Wargo, J. (2017). Hacking heteronormativity and remixing rhymes: Enacting a [q]ulturally sustaining pedagogy in middle grades English language arts. *Voices from the Middle, 24*(3), 39–43.

Whitin, P. (2002). Leading into literature circles through the sketch-to-stretch strategy. *The Reading Teacher, 55*(5), 444–450.

Willingham, D. T. (2009). *Why don't students like school?* San Francisco, CA: Jossey-Bass.

Wohlwend, K. (2009). Damsels in discourse: Girls consuming and producing identity texts through Disney princess play. *Reading Research Quarterly, 44*(1), 57–83.

Young, C. A. (2015, November). *The queer canon of children's literature: Reality represented or just another bully?* Research presentation for the Literacy Research Association Annual Conference, Carlsbad, CA.

Index

The letter *f* after a page number refers to a figure.

21st-century skills, 112–113
10,000 Dresses (Ewert), 93–95, 94f, 117, 121

About the book, 1, 11–16
Academic skills and standards, 112–113
Acceptance, 5, 7–8, 90–93
Accurate representations, 75, 96. *See also* Single-story representations; Stereotypes
ACLU (American Civil Liberties Union), 111
Adams, R., 5
Adichie, C. N., 84, 86–87
Administration, 38, 111–113
Advocacy groups, 108–109, 111
After-reading activities, 44
After Tupac and D Foster (Woodson), 96, 99–103, 105f, 106, 118, 122
Airton, L., 12
Allies. *See* LGBTQ allies
American Academy of Pediatrics, 6–7
American Civil Liberties Union (ACLU), 111
American Library Association, 109
Anchor lessons with straight texts
grade 3: racial divisions, 73–77
grade 4/5: gendered expectations, 73, 77–81
other development opportunities, 81–82

Androgyny, 93
And Tango Makes Three (Richardson & Parnell), 22, 117, 119, 121
Anti-harassment policies, 8, 110–111
Application of laws, 109
Applying learning, 11
Appropriateness of teaching topics, 31–32, 38, 114
A Queer Endeavor organization, 108
Assault, 110
Athanases, S., 12
Atkinson, E., 4, 12
Audio-visual representations. *See* Media representations
Authors of this book, 12, 13

Background knowledge. *See* Prior knowledge
Balanced selection of literature. *See* Mirror books and window books
Balf, R., 9
Banned Books Week, 109
Bartkiewicz, M. J., 8, 107–108
Because of Winn-Dixie (DiCamillo), 55, 62, 63–65, 121
Bednar, M., 13–14, 76, 89
Before-reading activities, 41–42, 77–78
Bell, J., 90
Bentley, D. F., ix
Be Who You Are (Carr), 93, 94–95
"Big ideas," 113

Binary categories, 58–60, 68, 77,
    78–80
Bishop, R. S., 20
Blackburn, M. V., 12, 35
Blaise, M., 4, 12
Blind Men and the Elephant, The, 85
Boesen, M. J., 8
Books with LGBTQ characters and
    themes, 3, 118–120, 121–122.
    See also by name; Expanding
    representations
Brill, S. A., 6
Britton, J., 10
Britzman, D., 57, 58, 60
Buckley, J. F., 12
Bullying, 3, 7–8, 17, 29–31, 45, 110,
    111–112
Butler, J., 57, 58, 59
Butler, S., 80

California Healthy Youth Act, 111
Casper, V., 12
Categories, 56, 57–59, 80–81. See
    also Connected categories;
    Heterosexual matrix
Censorship, 71, 109
Challenges. See Considerations for
    instruction
"Character dive," 104, 105f
Child development, 6–7
Choice to participate, 34–35, 114
Clark, C. T., 12, 35
Clarke, L., 69
Class discussion, 33, 42, 44, 49, 66, 69,
    77–78, 100
Class formats, 33
Classification, 58
Classroom context considerations. See
    Considerations for instruction
Classroom materials, 117–119
Classroom teachers featured in this
    book, 12, 13–14
Closeted, 6, 30

Clothing, 65, 67
Cohen, C., 87
COLAGE, 108
Color, 64
Combined approach. See Questioning-
    silences approach
Comfort level, 1, 2, 4, 5–6, 43, 107
Coming out, 6, 30
Communication, 11, 34, 111–112,
    113–114
Compare-and-contrast skill, 92, 93, 94,
    94f
Compassion, 31, 33, 92
Complicating categories. See
    Questioning-categories approach
Connected categories, 59–60. See also
    Heterosexual matrix
Connecting to experience. See Text-to-
    self connections
Connections between topics, 98
Considerations for instruction, 34–36,
    71–72, 109, 110
Constraints, 109, 110
Conversation. See Communication
Cowhey, M., 11
Crenshaw, K., 84, 87
Critical thinking, 86, 112–113
Crooked River (Pearsall), 39, 62,
    66–69, 121
Current events, 28–32, 33, 90, 98

Daniels, H., 10
Danischewski, D. J., 5, 6, 7, 8, 107–
    108, 113
Data collection and analysis, 14–15
Davies, B., 9
Davis, B., 12, 58, 60
Day of Silence, 108
DeMeules, M., 7
DePalma, R., 4, 12
Derogatory language. See Language:
    derogatory
Diaz, E. M., 107–108

Difference, 39–40, 44–45, 81, 83, 87, 91, 106
Discomfort. *See* Comfort level
Diversity, x, 1–2, 23–25, 90–92, 96–97, 112, 113
Dominant culture, 21
Donovan's Big Day (Newman), 22, 118, 121
"Don't Say Gay" law, 109
Dozier, C., 11
Dramatic interpretation, 49, 50–51
Drawing activities. *See* Sketch-to-stretch activity
Dress and gender, 65, 67
During-reading activities, 42–44
Durwood, L., 7
Dutro, E., 9, 10, 21
Dyson, A. H., 10

Each Kindness (Woodson), 80, 121
Early childhood education, ix, 108
ELA (English Language Arts) curriculum, 8–12, 104–106, 105f, 112
Emdin, C., 10, 21
Enciso, P., 10, 21
English Language Arts curriculum. *See* ELA (English Language Arts) curriculum
Enriquez, G., 69
Epstein, D., 12, 107
Equity, ix, x, 1, 113
Expanding-representations approach
  about, 17–18, 19–20, 37–39
  challenges, 34–36
  classroom practices, 32–34
  entry points: current events, 28–32
  entry points: personal experience, 23–28
  mirror books and window books, 20–23
  novel study: gay protagonist, 39–47
  novel study: transgender protagonist, 47–54

FAIR Education Act, 111
Familiar ELA practices, 32–34, 69–70, 95–96. *See also by activity*
Families with LGBTQ members, 5–6, 23–26
Family Equality Council, 108
Fear, ix, 2, 35, 107
Flint, A. S., 11
Flint, MI, water crisis, 98
Foucault, M., 57
Freedom, 68–69
Freire, P., 11, 73
Friendship, The (Taylor), 77, 122
Friendship for Today, A (McKissack), 39, 121

Gadsen, V., 9
Gates, G. J., 5, 6
Gatto, L., 11
Gender
  expression of, 90–93
  heterosexual matrix, 59–66, 71, 75–76, 77, 79, 112
  and identity, 6–7, 50, 52–53, 55–56, 93, 110–111
  and language, 48, 49, 51–52, 53, 62–63, 93, 94
  nonbinary identity, 90–92
  transgender identity, 3, 6, 76, 89–90, 93–94
  unwritten rules, 64, 65, 67, 73–77, 75, 79–80, 81–82
Gender creative, 90–92
Gender Spectrum, 108
Genishi, C., 10
George (Gino), 37–38, 47–53, 99, 113, 121
Giga, N. M., 5, 6, 7, 8, 107–108, 113
Glossaries, 120
GLSEN, 5, 6, 22, 108, 109, 111
Greytak, E. A., 5, 6, 7, 8, 107–108, 111, 113
GSA Network, 108

Harassment, 8, 110–111. *See also*
    Bullying
Harris, J., 6–7, 21
Harris, V., 10
Harris Interactive, 5, 6, 22
Harste, J. C., 97
Health education, 109. *See also* Sex
    education
Hermann-Wilmarth, J. M., ix, 6, 13,
    23, 26–27, 35, 53, 56, 60, 64, 70,
    77, 81, 84, 88
Heteronormative perspective. *See*
    Heterosexual matrix
Heterosexual matrix, 59–66, 71,
    75–76, 77, 79, 112
Hip-hop, 101–102
Homophobia, 31
Howe, J., 37
HRC (Human Rights Campaign), 108,
    111
Hughes, L., 98
Human Rights Campaign (HRC), 108,
    111

Identity and reading, 9–10
Inaccurate representations, 75, 96. *See
    also* Single-story representations;
    Stereotypes
Incomplete categories. *See* Inaccurate
    representations; Single-story
    representations; Stereotypes
Inflection in reading, 42
Infusion, 8–9
In Our Mothers' House (Polacco), 3,
    17, 19–20, 118, 121
Instructional constraints, 109, 110
Interpretation, 85
Intersectional perspective, 87–88
Introducing LGBTQ people through
    literature, 17–18. *See also*
    Expanding-representations
    approach
Is Your Family Like Mine?
    (Abramchik), 23, 121

Janks, H., 11
Jenkins, H., 96, 97
Johnston, P., 11
Jones, S., 9, 10, 21, 69
Justice. *See* Social justice

Kauffmann, G., 12, 26, 27, 28, 34
Kazemi, E., 9
Kehily, M. J., 4
Kenney, L. M., 12
Kidd, K., 60
Kilodavis family, 90
King and King (Nijland & de Haan),
    26–27, 118, 120, 121
Kosciw, J. G., 5, 6, 7, 8, 107–108, 111,
    113
Kull, R. M., 111
Kumashiro, K., 58, 87

Labels. *See* Categories; Connected
    categories; Heterosexual matrix
Ladson-Billings, G., 10
Language
    derogatory, 26–27, 29–30, 45–46,
        110
    and gender, 48, 49, 51–53, 62–63,
        93, 94
    lessons in, 69, 74, 92, 93–94, 95
    terms and usage, 8, 17, 22, 23, 44–
        47, 51–53, 62–63, 93, 100, 120
Lannen, R., 14, 53, 77
Larger-frame rationale, 112
Laws concerning LGBTQ-inclusive
    education. *See* LGBTQ-inclusive
    education: policies concerning
Layered identities. *See* Intersectional
    perspective
Learning focus, 112–113
Legal restrictions, 109, 110
Leibowitz, S. F., 6
Leonardi, B., 58
Lesson-plan links, 119–120
Lester, J. Z., 88
Letters to the author, 51–53

Letter writing, 104
Letts, W., 12
Lewison, M., 11
LGBTQ allies, 42, 45, 50–51, 80,
    108–109
LGBTQ-inclusive education. *See
    also* Expanding-representations
    approach; Questioning-categories
    approach; Questioning-silences
    approach
    about, ix–x, 1–2, 4, 5, 11–12, 13
    and critical literacy, 8–11
    pedagogical decision, 111–114
    policies concerning, 107, 108,
        109–111
    questions, 1–2
    rationale, ix–x, 2–8, 8–11, 111
    resistance to, 33, 35, 52, 113–114
    resources, x, 108–109, 117–120
    as a right and responsibility, ix–x,
        2–5, 114
Listening to parents, 113–114
Listening to students, 22–23, 25
Literary genre, 104, 105f
Literature response, 33
Local organizations, 108–109
Lorde, A., 84, 98
Luke, A., 9

Macedo, D., 73
Making meaning, 9–10, 32
Marginalization. *See* Difference
Marriage, 22
McLaughlin, K. A., 7
Media representations, 3, 28–29, 119
Media resources, 119
Meier, C., 6–7
Meyer, E., 12
Mirror books and window books,
    20–21, 33, 100
Misconceptions about LGBTQ people,
    ix, 2, 28
Misfits, The (Howe), 108
Misgendering, 49, 63

Modeling, 90
Modern Family, 3
Moje, E., 9
Morrell, E., 10
Multiple representations, 88–89
Multiple texts. *See* Text sets
My Princess Boy (Kilodavis), 83,
    90–95, 92f, 94f, 118, 121
Myths about LGBTQ people, ix, 2, 28

NAEYC (National Association for the
    Education of Young Children), x
National Association for the Education
    of Young Children (NAEYC), x
National Council of Teachers of
    English, 109
National School Climate Surveys,
    109–110
Negative language. *See* Language:
    derogatory
News. *See* Current events
No Name-Calling Week, 108
Nonbinary identity, 90–92
Nondiscrimination laws, 110
Nonparticipation. *See* Choice to
    participate
"No Promo Homo" law, 109, 110
Normalized behavior, 21, 25, 67–70
Novels list, 118
Novel studies
    gay protagonist, 39–47
    introduction, 37–39
    resources, 118, 119–120
    transgender protagonist, 47–54
Nuanced understanding, 85–86, 92, 96,
    101, 104

Objections to LGBTQ-inclusive
    teaching. *See* LGBTQ-inclusive
    education: resistance to
Office for Intellectual Freedom, 109
O'Grady, Barbara, 14
Olson, K. R., 7
Open-ended questions, 69

Other Side, The (Woodson), 73–74,
77–82, 122
Overview of this book, 15

Palmer, N. A., 8
Parent communication, 38, 111–114
Participation in instruction. *See* Choice
to participate
Patraw, J., 76, 89
Payne, E., 12
Pepper, R., 6
Persinger, J., 5
Picture book titles, 117–118
Pinar, W., 12
Poetry, 98
Policies concerning LGBTQ-inclusive
education. *See* LGBTQ-inclusive
education: policies concerning
Popular culture representations. *See*
Media representations
Power, 50–51, 58–59, 77, 78–79, 106
Power of story, 10
Prekindergarten, ix
Prewriting activities, 95
Primary grades, ix
Prior knowledge, 9–10, 33, 42, 106
Problem-solving theme, 39–40, 112
Professional development, 108
Professional educational organizations,
109

Queer Endeavor, A, 108
Queering categories. *See* Questioning-
categories approach
Questioning-categories approach
about, 55–58, 73–74
building a queer lens, 60, 70, 73, 77,
80–81, 83–84, 96
challenges, 71–72
continuing learning, 77–81
entry points: discussion
opportunities, 63–69
entry points: general, 61–62

entry points: oral language, 62–63
entry points: unwritten rules, 74–77,
81–82
familiar practices, 69–70
importance and nature of categories,
58–61
Questioning-silences approach
about, 73–74, 83–84, 98–99
challenges, 96–97
and ELA curriculum, 104–106, 105f
familiar practices, 95–96
intersectional identities, 99–103
representations, 85–88
using text sets, 88–95, 92f, 94f
Quinlivan, K., 12

Race, 20, 58–59, 77–81
Read-aloud process and activities,
41–44, 47–48, 69–70, 74–75, 78,
93, 100
Real-world connections, 11, 100
Recap, 41–42, 48
Reflective writing, 83, 90–92, 92f, 95,
101, 102–103
Relationships between characters, 28
Relevance of LGBTQ-inclusive
education, 2–3, 5
Renold, E., 4
Representations in literature. *See*
Mirror books and window books
Requirement to teach LGBTQ
information, 111
Research activity, 101, 102–103
Research for this book, 13, 14–15
Resources for LGBTQ-inclusive
education. *See* LGBTQ-inclusive
education: resources
Review-and-discuss process, 41–42, 48
Rich, A., 59
Rights, ix, x, 7, 29, 114
Robinson, K. H., 4, 12
Rogers, R., 11
Rosenblatt, L., 9

Rules. *See* Gender: unwritten rules;
LGBTQ-inclusive education:
policies concerning
Ryan, C. L., 4, 6, 13, 19, 20, 35, 53,
56, 60, 70, 76, 77, 81, 84, 88, 89

"Safe school laws," 110
Safety, 35, 50, 73, 110, 113
Schall, J., 12, 26, 27, 28, 34
Schema, 9–10
School administration. *See*
Administration
School climate and culture, 5, 8, 114–115
Schultz, S., 12
Sears, J., 12
Self-censoring, 5–6
Self-esteem, 20, 41
Sex education, ix, 2, 28, 109
Sexuality, 4, 59–60, 74, 77, 79, 81–82
Sexual orientation, 55–56, 110–111
Siegel, M., 97
Single-story representations, 84, 85,
86–87, 96. *See also* Stereotypes
Sipe, L., 37
Sketch-to-stretch activity, 24, 69, 80
Smith, J. M., 12
Smith, M. J., 12
Social justice, ix, x, 112
Souto-Manning, M., ix, 5, 6, 10, 13,
21, 23, 26–27, 34, 64
Spack, N. P., 6
Stacked categories, 56–60. *See also*
Heterosexual matrix
Staley, S., 58
Stereotypes, 42, 87, 96. *See also* Single-
story representations
Stories related to identity, 86–87
Straight texts. *See* Anchor lessons
with straight texts; Questioning-
categories approach
Street, B., 9
Substance Abuse and Mental Health
Services Administration, 7

Suicide, 29–31
Sumara, D., 12, 58, 60
Supporting pedagogical decisions,
111–114
Support sources, 107–109
Synthesis activity, 95

Tale of Despereaux, The (DiCamillo),
81–82, 121
Teacher education, 13, 108, 109
Teachers featured in this book, 12,
13–14
Teaching constraints, 109, 110
Terms and usage. *See* Language: terms
and usage
Text sets, 84, 89–90, 93, 95, 96, 99
Text-to-self connections, 43–44, 69,
91, 95
Text-to-text connections, 91, 92f, 94,
94f, 95
Themes, 101–103
Ticknor, A. S., 20
Tilland-Stafford, A., 12
Time pressure, 8, 96
Tokenism, 35–36, 96
Tolerance. *See* Acceptance
Totally Joe (Howe), 37, 39–47, 83,
89–93, 118, 121
Town, S., 12
Transacting meaning, 9–10, 32
Transgender identity. *See under*
Gender
Transitioning, 89–90, 93–94
Tschida, C. M., 20
Tyson, C., 10, 21

Units, 84
Unwritten rules. *See under* Gender
Using this book, 15–16

VanEvery, J., 4, 107
Van Sluys, K., 11
Vasquez, V., 5

Venn diagram, 94, 94f
Videos. *See* Media representations
Villenas, C., 5, 6, 7, 8, 107–108, 113
Vocabulary. *See* Glossaries; Language

Walker-Hoover, Carl Joseph, 29–32
Wallace, A., 4, 107
Wargo, J., 58
Welcoming behavior, 5
Welcoming Schools project, 108
Whitin, P., 69

Who's in a Family? (Skutch), 24, 122
Willingham, D. T., 97
Window books and mirror books. *See*
    Mirror books and window books
Wohlwend, K., 4
Woodson, J., 98
Writing extension activities, 51–53,
    103–106, 105f
Writing skills, 103–104

Young, C. A., 88

About the Authors

Caitlin L. Ryan is an associate professor of reading education in the College of Education at East Carolina University in Greenville, NC. She previously taught literacy enrichment programs to grades K–5 in the Washington, DC, Public Schools. Her research interests center on the relationships among children's literature, literacy, social positioning, and educational equity, especially at the elementary school level.

Jill M. Hermann-Wilmarth, a former elementary school teacher, is a professor of social foundations in the Department of Teaching, Learning, and Educational Studies at Western Michigan University in Kalamazoo, MI. Her research and teaching examine issues of identity inside and outside of classrooms using the lenses of literacy, social justice, and critical and deconstructive theories. She is currently at work on her first children's novel.

Caitlin and Jill have been researching, writing, and presenting together since 2007. Their article in the *Journal of Literacy Research*, "Already on the Shelf: Queer Readings of Award-Winning Children's Literature," was awarded the 2013 Article of the Year award from the American Educational Research Association's Queer Studies Special Interest Group. Their work can also be found in *Language Arts, Journal of Language and Literacy Education*, and *Discourse: Studies in the Cultural Politics of Education*, among other places.